Ancient Peoples and Places

JUGOSLAVIA
BEFORE THE ROMAN CONQUEST

General Editor

DR GLYN DANIEL

ABOUT THE AUTHOR

John Alexander was a student at the Universities of Cambridge and London, where he read History and Archaeology respectively. He was later awarded his doctorate at Cambridge for work on the Jugoslav Iron Age, after having held a Jugoslav Government Research Fellowship. He has since continued to work and publish on Jugoslav and Balkan problems, especially the spread of iron-using. During this time he has taught Prehistoric European Archaeology to under-graduate and adult students in the Universities of Cambridge and London and is at present Staff Lecturer in Archaeology in the Department of Extra-Mural Studies of London University.

JUGOSLAVIA
BEFORE THE ROMAN CONQUEST

John Alexander

54 PHOTOGRAPHS
70 LINE DRAWINGS
7 MAPS
I CHRONOLOGICAL TABLE

THAMES AND HUDSON

THIS IS VOLUME SEVENTY-SEVEN IN THE SERIES
Ancient Peoples and Places
GENERAL EDITOR: DR GLYN DANIEL

To Josip Korošec, scholar and teacher

First published 1972
© Thames and Hudson Ltd 1972
Filmset by Keyspools Ltd, Golborne, Lancs and
printed in Great Britain by Camelot Press Ltd, Southampton.
Not to be imported for sale into the U.S.A.
ISBN 0 500 02074 4

CONTENTS

List of Illustrations

Introduction

The last two decades in Jugoslavia have seen a greater increase in our knowledge of the long ages before the Roman Conquest than any previous period. All over the country, in universities, museums and national agencies excavation and research has been carried on and it has become possible, for the first time, to offer an outline history of man in this part of Europe. This has been helped by similar increases in knowledge in neighbouring countries, especially Hungary, Bulgaria and Romania.

In the last five years new ways of looking at the evidence, new methods of dating and excavation have meant that a critical reappraisal of the whole body of evidence has become desirable and, whilst it is too early to do more than indicate the direction which these new studies are taking under the second post-war generation of Jugoslav archaeologists, it is perhaps useful to set them down.

Present-day Jugoslavia, the Federal People's Republic of the Southern Slavs (Jugo-Slavs), is a recent political creation based on racial and linguistic realities, and it does not, on many of its frontiers, coincide with significant boundaries of physical geography. It is different, however, when the component republics, Slovenia, Croatia, Bosnia-Hercegovina, Serbia, Macedonia and Montenegro, are considered, for these are based on genuine and very ancient regions, something of whose individuality can already be seen in the prehistoric period. They share between them the main geographical regions of Jugoslavia: the Coastal Plains, Fjords and Islands of the Adriatic Sea (divided between Slovenia, Croatia and Montenegro); the Inland Watershed, the long series of mountain ranges which continue from the Eastern Alps of Austria to Greece (divided between Slovenia, Croatia, Bosnia-Hercegovina and Montenegro); the great plain and surrounding hills of the Middle Danube Basin (divided between Croatia and Serbia); and the Morava-Vadar Depression, which falls within Serbia and Macedonia.

Into the Danube, near the eastern frontier, drain the main Jugoslav rivers, the Drave, the Save with its great tributaries and the Morava.

Fig. 1

Fig. 1 Jugoslavia today, showing main cities, regional and national frontiers

Towards the Adriatic Sea on the southwest, only the River Naretva achieves more than local importance; while to the south, the River Vadar runs through Macedonia into Greece.

It is the pattern of communication imposed by the river systems and the mountains which has resulted in the strongly-marked individual characters of the present-day constituent republics. In the past this factor has often made it easier to trade, fight or unite with neighbours external

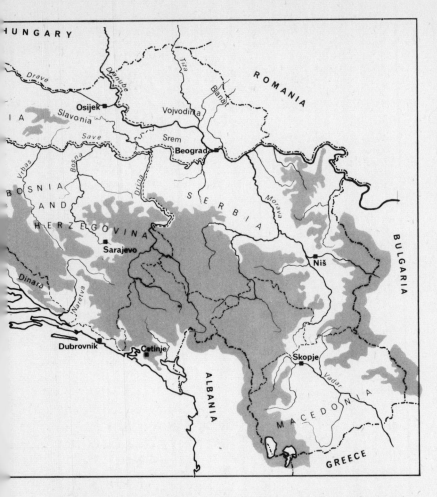

to the present federation than with neighbours inside it. Slovenia has always had close links with Central Europe (Austria and Czechoslovakia); Croatia and most of Serbia have looked north and east to the Danube Plains (Hungary, Romania and Bulgaria); whilst Macedonia and Montenegro have had close connections with the south and west (Greece and Albania). The Adriatic coastlands, although not one of the republics and now divided between Slovenia, Croatia and

Montenegro, have had in the past a unity as Dalmatia, accustomed to look across the sea, especially towards Italy and Greece.

THE BACKGROUND TO HUMAN OCCUPATION

Since the evidence about to be presented shows that man has lived in Jugoslavia for some two hundred thousand years, the changes in topography, climate, vegetation and animal life must be considered.

Geologically, the last two hundred thousand years fall within the later Pleistocene and the Holocene period. Both are relatively so recent and have been so free from major disturbance, that there has been little change in the physical geography of Jugoslavia. The pattern of coastal plain, north-south folded mountain ranges, and an inland plain through which most of the rivers flow north and east, must always have been man's frame of reference. The only major variations have been on the coast, where there was emergence of parts of the bed of the northern Adriatic Sea when sea levels fell in periods of intense cold, and an extensive 'drowning' of the coastal valleys when sea levels rose in periods much warmer than today.

The mountain ranges continue in the north the folding pattern of the eastern Alps, rising in the Julian Alps to 9,400 feet. As a result the main valleys along which flow the Save and Drave open southeastwards into the Danubian Plain; today the towns of Ljubljana and Maribor mark their emergence from the mountains.

Further south the fold-lines are more northwest to southeast and so the Velebit (Dinaric) Alps are parallel to the coast and rise in Mount Durmitor to 8,234 feet. These largely limestone mountains give rise to the typical 'Karst' landscape with little surface water, many caves and Plates 1, 2   solution hollows, and wide intermontane valleys. In Bosnia, Hercegovina and Montenegro the mountainous area widens out and covers several thousand square miles. This offers a natural refuge area in which ancient customs linger, and, as has been shown in recent years, a difficult problem to human would-be conquerors.

East of the mountains the Middle Danube Plain is the bed of the ancient Pannonian Lake overlaid in places by glacial or periglacial deposits of which wind-deposited loess is the most important. These fertile lowlands are well exemplified by the Srem district of Croatia and the Banat and Vojvodina of Serbia.

In southern Serbia and Macedonia, the depression which forms the basins of the Rivers Morava and Vadar is composed of broken, hilly country which distinguishes it from neighbouring regions.

Climatically the last two hundred thousand years have been varied, for two major glacial, and two major temperate phases can be recognized in the area. Although Jugoslavia was too far south and too low-lying to be covered at any time by ice-sheets, there were permanent snow and ice caps over some of the mountains during the glacial periods. The plant and animal evidence discussed below suggests that in none of these phases were the climates very different from those found in various parts of Europe at the present day.

The vegetation naturally changed during these successive phases, but since Jugoslavia has usually had adequate rainfall, and is generally low-lying, the changes have been chiefly between different kinds of forest. Occasionally the pattern has been varied in glacial phases by a spread of Tundra and Cold-Temperate Steppe floras. The forests – in succession Coniferous, Cool-Temperate Deciduous, Warm-Temperate Deciduous and Evergreen (Mediterranean) – can be shown to have contained the same kinds of trees (pine, oak, beech, etc.) as characterize them today. As the slow alternations of climate took place, so the frontiers of the tree- and plant-complexes must have varied and their animal inhabitants with them.

These animal populations were also very similar to those known in Europe today. Relatively few now-extinct species were present and the human inhabitants of Jugoslavia must have been familiar with red and roe deer, wild cattle, pig, goat and wolf for many millennia. Only during the earlier phases were certain species now unknown in the region, like elephant, rhinoceros and cave lion, found in any quantity there. In postglacial times the rivers and coasts were well stocked with fish.

In the whole period under consideration, therefore, the environments encountered by man presented him with no problems greater than those he has successfully solved in more recent times.

Mineral resources, which were important in the later periods of Jugoslav prehistory, included iron in Slovenia and Bosnia, where it is widespread and easily worked, copper in Bosnia and Serbia, and silver in Bosnia; gold occurred in the alluvial deposits of many rivers.

BC	Vadar-Morava Depression	Danube Basin
5000	Bitolj ←	*Starčevo* ———
	Vinča Tordoš	
4000	Porodin Vinča Bubanj	Pločnik ——— Tiszapolgar Bab
		← *Baden-Pecel* ———
3000		
	West Serbian Tumulus Culture Slatina	Baden-Kostolac Baden-Lasi Slavor
2000	Paraćin Urnfield	Pečica Mokrin/Periam Cultures Zuto Brdo (Pannonian)
	← Kličevac	Dubovac Bijelo Brdo Vattina
1000	Kumanovo horizon Trebenište	*Thrako-Cimmerians* *Scyth*
	DARDANI TRIBALLI *Greek Province* ROMAN PROVINCE	GETAE *Breuci* *Scordisci* MAEZOEI
I AD		DACIANS

Cultures and tribes in Jugoslavia after 5000 BC.
Immigrant groups are shown in italic, historically known tribes in small capitals

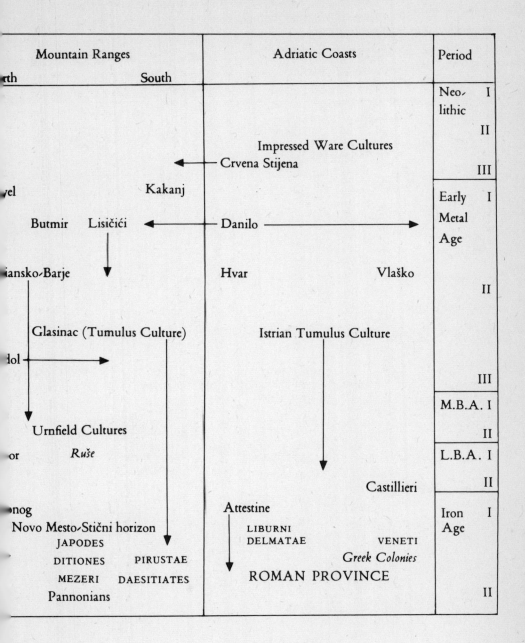

Mountain Ranges		Adriatic Coasts	Period
rth	South		

Neo-lithic I

II

Impressed Ware Cultures
Crvena Stijena

III

Kakanj — Early Metal Age I

vel

Butmir — Lisičići — Danilo

ansko-Barje — Hvar — Vlaško — Early Metal Age II

Glasinac (Tumulus Culture) — Istrian Tumulus Culture

lol

III

M.B.A. I

Urnfield Cultures

II

or — Ruše — L.B.A. I

Castillieri — II

nog — Attestine — Iron Age I

Novo Mesto-Stični horizon

JAPODES — LIBURNI

DITIONES — PIRUSTAE — DELMATAE — VENETI

Greek Colonies

MEZERI — DAESITIATES — ROMAN PROVINCE

Pannonians — II

15

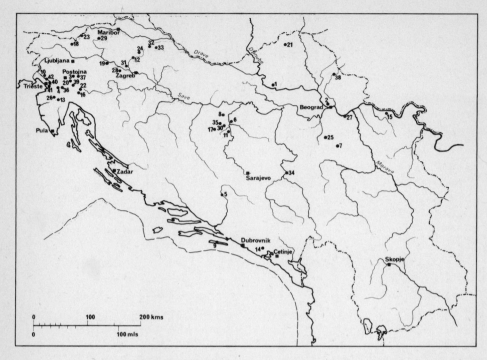

Fig. 2 Jugoslavia, showing Palaeolithic and Mesolithic sites. The broken line indicates the coastline during the Last Glaciation

1 Bačka Palanka
2 Batajnica
3 Betulov Spodmol
4 Crni Kal
5 Crvena Stijena
6 Doboj
7 Gradac
8 Grabovca brdo
9 Jezero, Malo
10 Jama, Pod Kalom
11 Kamen
12 Krapina
13 Kraške Spilje
14 Lipci
15 Lepenski Vir

16 Lovke Zijalka
17 Luščić
18 Mokriška Jama
19 Njivice Zijalka
20 Ovčja Jama
21 Peres (Hajdukova)
22 Pestnjak
23 Potočka Zijalka
24 Punikve kod Ivanča
25 Risovača
26 Skočjanska Jama
27 Smederevo
28 Samobor
29 Špehovka Zijalka

30 Usora
31 Veternica
32 Vilenica
33 Vindija Spilja
34 Višegrad
35 Visoko brdo
36 Vlaško Pecina
37 Zakajeni Spodmol
38 Žitiste
39 Zupanov Spodmol
40 Grotta Azzurra di
   Samartorza
41 Caverna della Trincea
42 Grotta della Gallerie

CHAPTER I

Hunters, Gatherers and Fishers of the Palaeolithic and Mesolithic Periods

In Jugoslavia, as over most of Europe, hunter/gatherer communities preceded for long ages of time all other kinds of societies. This stage of cultural evolution was contemporary with much of the Quaternary Period (the last two million years), and the communities living in the earlier part of it, the Pleistocene, are conventionally considered under the heading of Palaeolithic or 'Old Stone' Age.

THE PALAEOLITHIC PERIOD

The evidence of this period in Jugoslavia is still very limited, mainly because intensive field-work has been restricted to a few areas, and the map shows field-workers rather than patterns of ancient populations. At present almost a hundred sites are known from the country, but few have been published in detail and only a brief outline of their probable significance can yet be given. That significance is enhanced by a know-ledge of the different environments in which men found themselves in this long period.[1]

The physical geography of Jugoslavia in the Pleistocene period must have been similar to that of today, for the pattern of mountains, plains, river valleys and coasts described in the introduction was already present. At times, however, the slow fluctuations of climate caused at least three major physical deviations from present-day conditions. In the glacial periods, there was probably permanent snow in the mountains above 1,800 metres in the coastal areas and 1,200 metres in the interior.[2] This would have meant that in the mountains of western Jugoslavia there was, for long periods, a permanent snow cover which acted as a barrier between hunters on the coast and those of the interior, and between those of the Middle Danube Plain and those to the west, north and south.

Another physical change during glacial periods would have been in the Dalmatian coastline. When much water was locked up in the great ice-caps, sea levels fell and parts of the northern Adriatic sea-bed became dry land.[3] At times of the lowest sea levels there would have been a plain

Fig. 2

in the Istria-Dalmatia region as far south as Zadar, movement between Italy and Dalmatia would have been easy, and it is to be expected that the coastal hunter/gatherers there were culturally linked with the Italian ones as those of the interior were with Hungary and Romania.

A third physical change during glacial periods was the accumulation of loess (mostly wind-blown soil) near the flanks of the mountains. Soils formed on their surfaces during warm periods, thus providing a useful chronological series.[4]

During the warmer interglacial periods, the mountain ice-caps melted so that contact between the Middle Danube Basin and the Mediterranean Coast was possible, and the sea rose even above the present-day levels causing the coastal plains to be inundated. With the flooding of the coastal plains and the opening of the mountain passes, communication between the coastal and inland groups probably became easier while the cultural links with Italy were diminished.

Much is known of the flora and fauna of both temperate and arctic phases in the Later Pleistocene period and it seems that relatively few animals and plants have become extinct.

THE LOWER PALAEOLITHIC PERIOD (BEFORE *c.* 70,000 BC)

No archaeological material so far found in Jugoslavia can be dated with an certainty earlier than the third major glacial phase of the Alpine series, the 'Riss' glacial advances, which may be assigned to *c.* 200,000–100,000 BC. Earlier human occupation in the interior is however likely, for in neighbouring Hungary, at Verteszöllös, there was a human settlement with fires and a well-made flake-tool industry in the second (Mindel) major glacial phase which has been dated to *c.* 300,000 BC. In Romania, in the Olt Basin, simple pebble-tools may well belong to the even earlier 'Villefranchian' phase of the Pleistocene. In the absence of dating evidence the significance of finds of similar tools in Jugoslavia cannot be assessed, but pebbles struck to make a variety of chopper tools have been reported from Hrvatsko Zagorje, Punikve Kod Ivanca and Pestrijak, and hand-axes from Hrvatske Zagorje and Monastir.[5] Hand-axes of a somewhat similar kind are found in Western Europe in the period 200,000–100,000 BC.

The earliest datable evidence comes at present from caves and loess deposits. The sites suggest that in the Riss Glaciation the human groups who visited the mountains practised Levalloisian stone-flaking techniques using careful retouching similar to that used in the earlier (Buda) industry of Verteszöllös and in the later Mousterian industries of the region. To call them 'Proto-Mousterian' is probably justified and they may well be part of a long continued flake-using tradition in this region. The best evidence at present comes from two caves, Crvena Stijena and Betulov Spodmol, which were used by men at intervals over many millennia and therefore have long successions of stratified material. The most recently published, Crvena Stijena[6] lies on the side of a tributary valley of the Bosna and in nine metres of deposit the excavators, Basler and Brunnacker, recognized thirty-one levels. Level 24 was a thick

Fig. 3

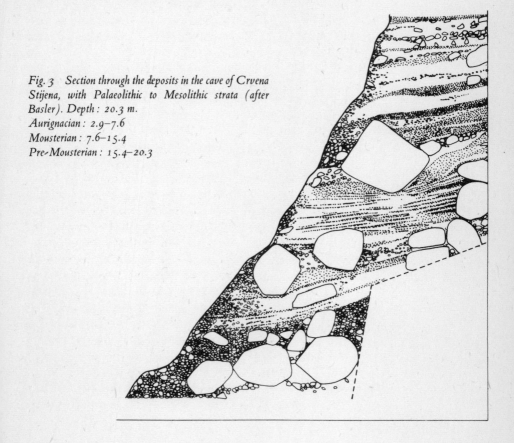

Fig. 3   Section through the deposits in the cave of Crvena Stijena, with Palaeolithic to Mesolithic strata (after Basler). Depth: 20.3 m.
Aurignacian: 2.9–7.6
Mousterian: 7.6–15.4
Pre-Mousterian: 15.4–20.3

interglacial deposit which on geological and zoological grounds belonged to early in the Last Interglacial period. The levels beneath it belonged to the previous (Riss) glaciation, and from them came an industry composed of small well-struck Levalloisian flakes some of which had small areas of unifacial retouch while others had been worked to form points.

The second site at Betulov Spodmol near Postojna also commands a valley which acts as a game funnel, and in the fourteen metres of deposit eleven major levels were distinguished.[7] The lowest, three metres thick and consisting of sharp-edged rock fragments produced by frost erosion, contained tools made by carefully retouching Levalloisian flakes and cave-bear bones. Stratified above was a thick sterile layer and then one of Last Interglacial date containing a Mousterian industry and a temperate fauna. Brodar, the excavator, suggested a 'Riss' glaciation date for the earliest level and called the tools Proto-Mousterian. Similar material has also been claimed from Spehovka, Njivic, Crnikal and Jama kod Kalon.

Evidence from the next period, the Last (Eemien) Interglacial ending *c.* 65,000 B C is more plentiful and is found on both sides of the mountains, which during this time would have lost their permanent snow-cap. The most important is at Krapina, 25 km from Zagreb. Here a rock shelter in a sandstone cliff high on the side of a tributary valley of the Drave had eight metres of accumulation, the bottom six being sealed by a stalagmitic concretion.[8] There seems to be little doubt that the sealed levels belong to the Last Interglacial phase. In the lowest level were found a hearth, a stone industry and human skeletal remains. The latter comprised some 600 pieces including 270 teeth and 11 jaws. The remains of at least 13 men, women and children were identified and among these 5 skulls were complete enough for detailed study. Day suggests that they were 'generalised neanderthalers', for some of their traits, particularly those of the teeth, were shared with *Homo sapiens neanderthalensis* but their similarities with modern man (*Homo sapiens sapiens*) have also been stressed.[9] These were not simple burials for most of the bones were broken and some of them were burnt; cannibalism has naturally been suggested but the evidence is not clear. With the human remains were found stone artifacts and industrial debris made from a variety of local rocks: flint, chalcedony, jasper, quartz. All the tools were made from flakes, the Levallois technique being frequently used.

Plates 3, 4

The retouch, of Mousterian type, was mostly used to make single-edge 'scrapers', but one or two tools had bifacial working and there were a few blade flakes. The tools were found with a temperate fauna which included wild cattle, beaver, cave-bear, red deer and an extinct species of rhinoceros (*R. merkii*) widely found in Europe in interglacial times.

At the two caves already mentioned some other artifacts were contemporary with those of Krapina. At Betulov Spodmol a flint industry with a temperate fauna lay below Early Last Glaciation remains and was placed in the Last Interglacial by Brodar, and at Crvena Stijena another was, on more definite grounds, similarly placed. Both were flake industries using Levalloisian techniques.

These industries may be linked with their contemporaries in Hungary and Romania and, in the case of Betulov Spodmol, with Italy.

Skull fragments with artifacts having similarities with the Krapina finds, have also been claimed from Bački (Petrovac) and Žitište (Vojvodina).

THE MIDDLE PALAEOLITHIC PERIOD (*c.* 70,000–*c.* 40,000 BC)

From the early part of the Last Glaciation (*c.* 70,000–40,000 BC), many sites with Middle Palaeolithic or 'Mousterioid' industries have been found in caves and open-air sites scattered through the mountains and foothills on both sides of the main watershed. Somewhat similar industries have been found in other parts of Europe associated with *Homo sapiens neanderthalensis* (Neanderthal Man) but in Jugoslavia only one certain fragment of this sub-species, a tooth from Gradac (Kragujevac), has been found.

Mousterian Industries In Slovenia and Bosnia regional variations with chronological significance have been claimed. In northern Bosnia, Basler saw a local distinction between Typical Mousterian industries made mainly on Levalloisian flakes and including unifacial points and side-scrapers, and a Later Mousterian with much more miscellaneous retouching, irregular tool forms and some bifacially worked points.[10]

In Slovenia, Brodar found two successive industries at Betulov Spodmol, the lower being a Mousterian-of-Levallois-Tradition but with a number of end-scrapers on flakes, and the upper a Developed Mousterian with many blade flakes.[11] An 'Alpine' Mousterian based more on locations than on tool assemblages has also been claimed.

21

Although none of the industries found has yet been considered statistically, and they are too far from the well-known West European groups for close parallels to be looked for, Bordes' 'Mousterian-of-Levallois-Tradition' and 'Micro-Mousterian' seem closest. To the east there are many parallels with the Mousterian and Szeletian industries of Hungary and Romania. Only in the Trieste region is there some evidence of a 'Mousterian-of-Acheulian-Tradition'.

Caves and rock shelters have provided the best detail, especially at Crvena Stijena, Betulov Spodmol, Risovača, Ovčja Jama, Zupanov Spodmol, Zakajeni Spodmol, Pocala and Vilenica. At Crvena Stijena the remains were sealed under a stalagmitic layer and the industry was composed of small flint and chert Clactonian and Levalloisian flakes made into simple edge-scrapers, some markedly convex, and a few points. Small pebbles were retouched to make scrapers and a few blade-flakes were made. At Betulov Spodmol, two successive industries were dated to this period. Both were found with rhinoceros (*R. merkii*), hyaena (*Ry. spelaeus*), wolf and marmot bones, whilst oak, elm, lime and poplar grew nearby. The lower industry was made from small flint and porphyry nodules flaked mainly by the Levalloisian technique and retouched into side-scrapers and points; some blade flakes were retouched

Fig. 4 Veternica; plan and section of the walled-up recesses containing bear bones (after Müller Karpe)

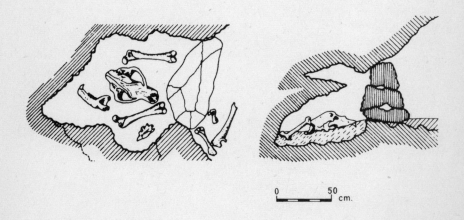

0   50
      cm.

to form end-scrapers. The upper industry, that described as 'Developed Mousterian', had more blade flakes, many retouched along one edge or at the end. Both these sites lie high in the mountains and in a glacial phase can only have been used as summer camps. At Risovaca a similar industry has been compared to the 'La Quina' Mousterian of western Europe, but had also some Hungarian (Szeletian) traits. It may have been rather later in date than the other finds for it was stratified above a conglomerate of early Wurm date. At Veternica, there was possible evidence of a religious cult which used cave-bear bones.

Open-air finds have mostly been in river terraces and on scree slopes in the mountains, but nowhere yet has a land surface on which men lived been identified. Visoko Brdo and Usora may be used to illustrate the types of site; at Visoko Brdo a Mousterioid industry was stratified beneath an Upper Palaeolithic 'Aurignacian' industry, and at Usora was mixed with one.

Fig. 4

In the limestone mountains of west Slovenia especially in the Postojna and Trieste regions, caves are very numerous, and there is little doubt that when this area has been intensively studied it will be as important in Jugoslavian, as the Dordogne region is in French, prehistory.

Open-air finds have mostly been in river terraces and on scree slopes in the mountains, but nowhere yet has a land surface on which men lived been identified. Visoko Brdo and Usora may be used to illustrate the types of site; at Visoko Brdo a Mousterioid industry was stratified beneath an Upper Palaeolithic 'Aurignacian' industry, and at Usora was mixed with one.

THE UPPER PALAEOLITHIC PERIOD (*c.* 40,000–*c.* 8000 BC)

The latest period of the Pleistocene, the 'later Würm' phase of the Alpine Glaciations, was remarkable throughout Europe for the appearance and continuing evolution of blade industries associated with the physical remains of *Homo sapiens sapiens* (Modern Man). Whilst these artifacts and bones have not been reported in association with skeletal remains in Jugoslavia, a scatter of blade industries through the country suggests that modern man was present during this period.

Many details of the climate, flora and fauna of this period are known. From Mljet in Dalmatia there are four forest periods, whilst from Slovenia, pollen from a series of borings in the marshes south of Ljubljana has shown alterations in the cold steppe and forest vegetations during the Later Würm period.[12] The same alterations are suggested by the varying species of animals, especially reindeer, horse and red deer, recorded in successive cave deposits at Pocala, Gabrovizza and Poštojna. Further south in Serbia, at Smederevo and Batajnica, layers of loess deposited under arctic conditions are separated by soils which mark the warmer periods (Interstadials) of the Würm Glaciation;[13] the soils suggest that cold steppe conditions often prevailed.

From the caves of the southern mountains, as at Crvena Stijena, come red deer, wild cattle and goat bones at this time.

Traditionally three groups of industries have been distinguished typologically, using the western European names of 'Aurignacian', 'Gravettian' and 'Magdalenian', but the similarites are not great enough for them or others like 'Olschewian' to be used with any precision. The finds, coming both from caves and from sites in the open air can only be dated from their stratigraphical positions and their associated animal bones, there being, as yet, no absolute (C14) dates published.

Aurignacian Industries Those labelled Aurignacian are the most wide-spread and perhaps the oldest, being found over the whole area; one is stratified below a 'Gravettian' industry at Kamen and another less certainly at Vindja Spilja, Varaždin. Although few detailed studies have yet been published, the general characteristics of the industries link them with western Romania and Hungary. From the stratigraphy in the cave excavations a development within these industries has been recognized.[14] At Betulov Spodmol a long succession (levels 24–12) of temporary, probably seasonal, occupations was noted, interrupted by a roof fall or a period of abandonment. Cave-bear and marmot, among other animals, were hunted with split-based bone spear-points and then dismembered and processed with carinated flint end-scrapers and backed-blades. Later, 'Developed' Aurignacians used bone spear-points with cut-sockets and very small (2 cm.) blades. Some of the blades were retouched into circular scrapers. Further south, in the cave of Crvena Stijena, a similar series of Aurignacian occupations was interrupted by a layer of redeposited limestone. Here the industries were associated with red deer, wild cattle and goat bones. As these caves and Mokriška Jama are high in the mountains it is likely that, as at Kokkinopolis in northern Greece, the occupations represent summer hunting expeditions. Lovke and Potocka Zijalka, perhaps belonging to the Olschewian group, should date to *c.* 30,000 BC.[15]

Other sites have been found in the open, the cluster in the Lower Bosna Valley representing the field-work of Basler. These are also likely to be temporary hunting stations, and from the animal bones in the same deposits belong to Late Würm glacial phases. The only site with

Fig. 5   Rock art from Lipci. Approx. actual size (after M. Garašanin)

internal stratigraphy was Kamen where, in a scree slope, 'Gravettian' were stratified above 'Aurignacian' remains.

Gravettian Industries   East Gravettian (Pavlovian) industries are widespread on the East European plains and surrounding mountains where they were often associated with mammoth (*E. primogenius*) hunting. The stone industries are distinguished by spear or lance points which were sometimes tanged and by distinctive backed blades and burins. Figurines of bone, ivory and other materials were often made. In Jugoslavia industries with some of these traits have been found.

Parallels have been noted between these finds and the Gravettian industries of Romania and Italy, and it seems possible that the route by which 'Gravettians' reached North Italy was through northern Jugoslavia. The most northerly well-stratified sites are near Trieste and Poštojna. At Ovoja Jama seven successive phases of Gravettian development were recorded with bone and other organic evidence and at Zupanov Spodmol and Azzura di Samatorza, Gravettian and later developments (Epi-Gravettian) were also well stratified.[16]

Further south some of the most interesting sites are neighbouring ones in northern Bosnia: Visoko Brdo, which is claimed as belonging to the Würm 1–2 interstadial (*c.* 40,000–30,000 BC), Lušćić and Kamen. Besides the backed blades mentioned above there was here a tendency, as at Zupanov Spodmol, to use very small fragments (microliths) for composite tools and weapons. Several collections of Gravettian artifacts have also been made in Montenegro, so that these industries are spread over the whole country. No figurines of the kinds made by Gravettians elsewhere have been found in Jugoslavia.

Magdalenian-type industries have been reported from Vindija (level 3) and Lokve,[17] but it is doubtful whether these should be linked with the industries of that name in Western Europe.

Few of the caves have yet revealed carvings or paintings which belong to this period, but the extent and number of them makes it quite possible that others await discovery. The most recent find of carvings, of stylised deer and subrectangular shapes, was made at Lipci.[18]

Fig. 5

Local transitions to the industries of the post-Pleistocene period may have been found. In the north, just over the Italian border at Azzura di Samatorza, a flint industry with some microliths was found below a shell-collecting culture of post-glacial (Mesolithic) type. Not far away in Zupanov Spodmol, Epi-gravettian remains of final or perhaps immediately post-Würm date also suggest the transition to the postglacial industries. Farther east and south at Kraške Spilje and Crevena Stijena a similar succession has been observed.[19]

THE MESOLITHIC PERIOD (*c.* 8000–6000 BC)

The hunter-gatherer-fisher cultures of postglacial (Early Holocene) times, although rather unfortunately named 'Mesolithic' or Middle Stone Age, were a direct continuation of the Palaeolithic tradition. That way of life ended only when its followers became agriculturists or pastoralists, or when they were displaced by immigrant farmers. During the three or four thousand years during which the Mesolithic communities may be presumed to have flourished, the topography, climate, flora and fauna of Jugoslavia became much as they are today. With the melting of the permanent snow cap of the Dinaric Alps, east-west movement became easier whilst with the rise in sea level, the present 'drowned' Dalmatian coastline developed and movement along the coast became more difficult. Since cool-temperate deciduous and warm-temperate evergreen forest floras had survived in southern Jugoslavia through the last glacial period, the re-colonisation of the country by such trees must have been rapid, causing much of the plains and hills to be soon covered; only in the mountains would coniferous forests have survived. In parts of the Middle Danubian Plain there were probably already regions of grassland

and here and there on hillsides and open spaces, the ancestors of domesti-
cated wheat, barley, oats and rye would have flourished among the other
grasses. Within the forests and on the mountains lived the animals that
are still native to the region, in particular deer, wild cattle, pigs and goats.

One other factor must be kept in mind when considering this period.
Throughout it, the domestication of some of the plant and animal species
native to Jugoslavia is known to have been taking place only a few
hundred miles away in western Asia, and it is not impossible that the
Balkans, including southern Jugoslavia, shared in the initial exper-
iments. It is also possible that some of the new ideas and techniques
arrived before farming became common in the sixth millennium (p. 33).

As in Europe generally, some of the Pleistocene hunters and gatherers
in Jugoslavia successfully adapted themselves to the new climatic
conditions, for the distribution of sites suggests that there were men living
in all parts of the country.

The stone industries found have been given the conventional western
European names of Azilian and Tardenoisian, but this must be taken
as giving no more than a general indication of their nature. So far only
microlithic industries (those using very small fragments of stone) have
been recognized; none had the heavy wood-working tools developed
further north in Europe by forest-dwellers.

A great limitation to the study of this period is that no absolute (C14)
dates for any period before the sixth millennium have yet been published,
and since microliths continued to be used by the earliest farmers in this
region (p. 35) some of the undated hunter-gatherer industries might well
be contemporary with them. Only from stratified sites and from
typological studies can the continued occupation of the country through
the whole period be suggested.

Continuity with late Palaeolithic (Epi-Gravettian) traditions has
been plausibly suggested for flint industries in western Slovenia, such as
those at Kraške Spilje and Zupanov Spodmol. In this they resemble the
neighbouring North Italian series. Two burials at Jama na Dolech in
the same region might also belong to this era; the bodies, fully *Homo
sapiens sapiens* in type, were covered with red ochre and had bone and
antler points and microlithic flint fragments with them.

In the mountains from southern Slovenia to Montenegro, other
hunter-gatherer groups flourished, preying on much the same animals

Fig. 6   Lepenski Vir I; a reconstructed house (after Srejović)

Fig. 3

as their Palaeolithic forebears, but using new microlithic equipment. The best stratified remains have come from the caves of Betulov Spodmol (layer 3) and Crvena Stijena (level 4). At the former, 1.10 m. of occupation debris of this period was separated by a thick sterile layer from palaeolithic remains, and by another sterile layer cemented with redeposited limestone, from the remains of early Neolithic farmers (p. 38). In spite of this, suggestions of typological continuity have been made. The associated animal bones incuded those of red deer and wild pig. The presence of geometric microliths, including trapezes, has led to the flint industry being described as Tardenoisian, and to a sixth or fifth millennium date being suggested.[20] At Crvena Stijena (layers 4–6) microlithic remains were also found below, and separate from, Neolithic debris. The crescentic, blunted-back blades and non-geometric forms from this site have led to it being compared with Baile Herculane in Romania and labelled Azilian. In the Slovenia mountains collections of microliths of similar type have come from caves like Kraške Spilje, Skocijanka Jama, and Vlaško Pecine, but their dates and stratigraphical positions seem uncertain.

A number of open-air sites have also been recognized, mostly in river terraces or in loess deposits. A concentration in northern Bosnia once again implies no more than intensive searching study in the Doboj region. In the Middle Danube plain one site has recently been located in loess at Peres (Hajdukova) in Serbia. Here there were microliths associated with a postglacial fauna, which included wild pig, ass and goat.[21] It has been described as Tardenoisian and might well indicate one kind of community present when the first farmers arrived.

The variety and richness of the new postglacial food resources enabled some groups to specialise in particular kinds of gathering and fishing. The best evidence comes at present from the shores of the Adriatic and the banks of the Danube. Stratified beneath neolithic remains in the cave of Azzura di Samatorza near Trieste was much microlithic debris including burins. In the lower levels land animals, especially red deer, were hunted but in the upper there were thick deposits of mussel and other shell fish.[22] These suggest an intensified use of the new food available from the warmer seas. A similar deposit came from the Cavernetta della Trincea and there are other (undated) shell middens near the Lerne Canal in Istria which might derive from this period.

Lepenski Vir Culture   A specialized inland culture has also been claimed in Serbia at Lepenski Vir. This lies east of Belgrade (Beograd) near the beginning of the gorges of the Danube known as the 'Iron Gates'. In a recess in the bank reached only by a narrow passage along the face of the cliff and facing a whirlpool, the remains of eight successive settlements divided into three main phases have been excavated.[23] The lowest level was stratified under the remains of Neolithic farmers and has radiocarbon dates of between 5100 and 4500 BC. It has been named the Lepenski Vir Culture and was a settled and well-established fishing, hunting and probably gathering community. There was no evidence of agriculture or of stock-breeding and most of the animal bones found were those of red deer and wild pig; fish bones were common and were of many river species, including sturgeon.

Plates 5–8

Fig. 7   Plan of the settlement at Lepenski Vir (after Srejović)

Figs. 6, 7   The settlement, in which five building horizons could be recognized, was scattered over most of the available area. The houses, set in hollows, were irregular parallelograms of up to 5.5 × 3 m. with several hearths sunk into each floor; the floors, and possibly the wood and stone walls, being plastered and sometimes painted. The debris on these floors included much flaked stone and worked bone. Some of the most interesting finds were fifty-four sculptured boulders which were in, or scattered in front of, several houses but were concentrated around one in particular. Some were sculpted into animal forms, some simply had linear designs, but most were human heads. The radiocarbon dates suggest that this culture was in part, at least, contemporary with nearby farming communities (p. 34), and might be a specialized seasonal facies of them.

CHAPTER II

Stone-using Farmers

At present there is no reason to suggest that Jugoslavia was part of that area where the earliest domestication of plants and animals took place. The Jugoslavian evidence must therefore be considered in the light of three factors: the neighbouring regions where farming is known to have been practised earlier, the routes along which ideas and/or people travelled, and the indigenous hunter/gatherer/fisher groups among whom these ideas and/or people must have penetrated.

Farming in neighbouring Romania and Greece in the sixth millennium BC was already an efficient mixed economy based on wheat and barley, sheep/goats and pigs. Besides their distinctive way of life, these farmers had highly individual stone, clay and bone crafts.[1]

There are several routes along which ideas and people might have travelled northwards into Jugoslavia. In the centre of the region in Macedonia the Vadar and Morava Valleys, with a pass between them at the watershed, lead from the Aegean direct to the Middle Danube plain, and it is in the Aegean coastal plains near the Vadar Valley that some of the earliest Greek neolithic sites, including Nea Nikomedia, have been found. Other routes lead through the mountains on either side of the Vadar-Morava Valleys. Further east in Romania and Bulgaria there are several passes through the Carpathian mountains into Transylvania, although the route by water through the Danube gorges (the 'Iron Gates') is impracticable. Further west there are also ways through the mountains and beyond them the sea routes from western Greece and southern Italy to the Dalmatian coasts. Most of Jugoslavia, therefore, lies across or beside the routes which ideas and people must have taken if they were travelling northwards.

The non-farming inhabitants of Jugoslavia from 8000–6000 BC have already been considered (p. 26). They were familiar with wild cattle, pig, horse and goat, and probably, since these were around them, with wild seed-bearing grasses of the wheat, rye, oat and barley families. It is possible that some groups of these hunter/gatherer/fishers who were affected by the new ideas have already been recognized, although, as at Lepenski Vir, there is no reason at present to see any of them as earlier

Fig. 8

31

Fig. 8 Selected Neolithic sites in Jugoslavia

1 *Anzebegovo*	24 *Grgur Tumba*	47 *Predionica*
2 *Arnautovići*	25 *Hrtkovci*	48 *Porodin*
3 *Bapska (Vukovar)*	26 *Jablanica*	49 *Priština*
4 *Banjica*	27 *Jama na Dolech*	50 *Ptuj*
5 *Bitolj*	28 *Jama kod Kalom*	51 *Samatovci*
6 *Botoš*	29 *Jama Predjamskin*	52 *Šuplja Stena*
7 *Bordoš*	30 *Kakanj*	53 *Smilčić*
8 *Bubanj*	31 *Kruscica*	54 *Starčevo*
9 *Butmir*	32 *Kormadin*	55 *Subotica*
10 *Crnokalačka Bara*	33 *Kozluk*	56 *Tečić*
11 *Crvena Stijena*	34 *Krk*	57 *Valac*
12 *Danilo Gornje*	35 *Lepenski Vir*	58 *Vinkovci*
13 *Divostin*	36 *Lisičići*	59 *Vinča*
14 *Donja Klakar*	37 *Mali Losinj*	60 *Vlaško Jama*
15 *Donja Mahala*	38 *Matejski Brod*	61 *Vršnik*
16 *Drulovka*	39 *Mujevine*	62 *Vučedol*
17 *Gladnice*	40 *Nebo*	63 *Zarkovo*
18 *Gornja Tuzla*	41 *Niš*	64 *Zelena Pećina*
19 *Grabak*	42 *Novi Seher*	65 *Zelenikovo*
20 *Grapčeva Spelje*	43 *Obre*	66 *Grotta Azzurra di Samartorza*
21 *Grabovac*	44 *Obrež*	67 *Grotta della Gallerie*
22 *Gradac*	45 *Pavlovac*	68 *Grotta Gabrovizza*
23 *Gračanica*	46 *Pločnik*	

than the first immigrants. The 'non-ceramic neolithic' found at Subotica with a microlithic flint industry and curved unbaked clay fragments of possible bowl forms might represent something of this kind.[2] Other flint industries which suggest some changes from those of known hunter/gatherer traditions have been found at Grotta della Gallerie and Crvena Stijena (level IVa). Tringham, in a recent study of these industries, has however concluded that there is little evidence of contact between them and the first immigrant farmers.[3] Some of the early pottery-using groups may also belong to indigenous groups.

The climate of southern Jugoslavia was then, as now, of a warm-temperate type, similar to that of northern Greece. Much of the plains must have been covered by forests of evergreen, giving place on the mountain-sides to deciduous and coniferous trees. The spread of farming practice, therefore, can have had few obstacles except sociological ones, either for immigrants or indigenous peoples.

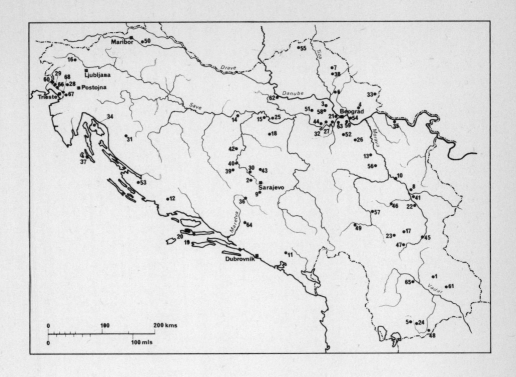

The long period of perhaps three thousand years during which farmers in Jugoslavia used stone for their tools falls into three subperiods: I, the earliest farming communities (before *c.* 4500 BC); II, the spread of farming ideas through northern Jugoslavia; III, the development and consolidation of regional cultures (after 4000 BC).

PERIOD I: THE FIRST FARMERS

THE EARLY NEOLITHIC PERIOD (*c.* 6000–4500 BC)

The evidence of the earliest of a sequence of northward movements comes from Jugoslav Macedonia where, near the Greek border, settlements of farmers may have preceded the Starčevo Culture discussed below. At Vršnik (Level 1) and Amzibegovo, the pottery, nail-impressed, monochrome, or more rarely decorated with white or red paint, is different from, and stratified below, that of the better known Starčevo Culture and has close parallels in Greek Macedonia. It should belong

33

in the sixth millennium BC and so mark one of the early movements northwards through the Vadar-Morava Valleys.

Starčevo Culture The first evidences of extensive farming settlements north of Macedonia have been named the Starčevo Culture. This was in existence at least as early as the late sixth millennium, and was the most south-westerly of a series of contemporary cultures: the Karanovo in Bulgaria, the Körös in southern Hungary and the Criş in Romania, which were responsible for the first exploitation of the Middle and Lower Danube Basins. All were restricted to areas south of the 41st parallel of latitude with warm-temperate climates. The Starčevo sites are concentrated on the loess-covered plains of the Banat and Vojvodina in northern Serbia,[4] where more than eighty of them are now known. The most westerly are at Gornja Tusla, Obre and Varos in north Bosnia and Vučedol in Croatia, but there seems to have been no penetration of the mountains or of the Upper Save and Drave Basins.

Many of the sites for settlement were chosen with such care, and the efficiency of the farmers was such, that they remained in use for many hundreds, sometimes thousands, of years. As a result the remains are found on stratified sites, some of them similar to the 'tells' of western Asia, and detailed absolute and relative chronologies are known. The general evidence from the Middle Danube Valley supports the view that farming was introduced by a slow northward movement which, when the rich loess deposits of the Middle Danube Basin were reached, gave rise to an increase in population probably with some integration of the local hunter/gatherers.[5]

The economy of the long-occupied 'tells', such as Amzibegovo, Porodin, Gornja Tuzla, Vršnik, Pavlovce and Starčevo, was a well-balanced agriculture similar to that of the earlier Aegean sites. Among the crops, wheat (einkorn, emmer and breadwheat) was important, but barley, millet, beans and vetches were also grown, and cattle, pigs and some sheep and goats were kept. Hunting and fishing varied in importance at different sites but at Kozluk, Lepenski Vir and Starčevo, for example, there were many deer and fish bones, the deer perhaps having been hunted at Kozluk with bone points. There is as yet no detailed published analysis of the animal bones from any site.[6]

At settlements like Vršnik, Zelenikovo, Lepenski Vir and Gračanica actual remains, and at Pavlovce models, of houses were found. Most,

Fig. 9   Clay figurine in Nandris' 'Rod style', from Obrež (after Brukner)

except at Lepenski Vir (Period II), were rectangular and built of wood, wattle and mud plaster. The individual rooms measured about 10× 6 metres and, in a number of cases, the floors were sunk below ground level. Domed clay ovens were found at Vršnik and Lepenski Vir (Period III). The models show the houses to have been gabled, with animal skulls on the ends of the ridge-poles. In size and construction they were similar to the houses at Karanovo in Bulgaria and Sesklo in Greece. If the size of the tells is significant, the settlements did not cover more than a few acres, but at Lepenski Vir there were at least forty houses in this period. So far none have been discovered with defences, although some are on hill-tops.

The few burials of dolicocephalic (long-headed) people found were almost all isolated inhumations in ditches or between houses. One collective grave of six people was discovered at Lepenski Vir.

The equipment in these settlements also linked the inhabitants with their neighbours in Greece and Romania. The ground-stone tools, the first found in Jugoslavia, include shoe-last adzes, and many small tri-angular axes, some with grooves. Flaked-stone tools were common from the earliest levels at most sites and included, especially at Kozluk, microlithic cores and microliths. Large blades, however, were the commonest form and were steeply retouched into end-scrapers, burins, points and sickle-blades. Whilst similar forms are found farther south on Greek sites, so much microlithic flint-work is not common, and might be evidence of the influence of local hunter/gatherers. Obsidian (natural volcanic glass) was known and was imported from Hungary. Other kinds of new equipment included bone needles, spoons, spatulas and prickers, clay loom-weights, spindle whorls, figurines and stamp-seals.

The few human and animal figurines found deserve separate comment. The finds come broken from the settlement debris and have no certain religious associations. They have a 'rod' form of body without limbs, a special emphasis on the moulding of the head, and most of the detail, except the 'coffee bean' eyes, is shown by incisions. The whole technique is more appropriate to stone- or wood- than clay-working.[7] They are similar to the figurines found in Anatolia and Greece, some being especially close to those from Nea Nikomedia.

Fig. 9

Pottery is now used in large quantities and provides much new evidence. Its variety, and the stratigraphy of the settlements, has allowed

Fig. 10 Starčevo II pot from Vincovči (after Dimitrejević). c. 1 : 4

Fig. 11 Starčevo III pottery from Vučedol (after Dimitrejević). c. 1 : 4

D. Garašanin, whose analysis is followed here, to subdivide it into three phases.[8]

The earliest phase, Starčevo I, which should belong to the late sixth millennium, was well-represented at Gornja Tusla (level VIb), Amzibegovo and Lepenski Vir (level II), and consisted of much finely burnished but coarse, sand- and straw-tempered brown, yellow and red pottery. These coarse wares, especially in southern Serbia, were ornamented by short incised lines, by finger impressions and by applied cordons. Flat-bottomed, pedestalled and four-legged bowl and cup forms were found. Fine, plain, monochrome ware of various kinds was also present.

Fig. 12

It has been suggested that the few figurines, the pottery tables (as from Gladnice and Zelenikovo) and some of the pots decorated with human faces may have had religious significance.

Burials from this phase are rare, but at Tešić two successive contracted burials were found with two fine bowls, one pedestalled. Similar burials were found at Lepenski Vir, one with a necklace.

The southern connections of this phase have been much studied.[9] A complex of traits link Greek Macedonia and southern Hungary via the Vadar and Morava Valleys. These included grooved, triangular and shoe-last axes and adzes, bone spoons, clay stamp-seals, 'rod-headed' figurines and horned pendants. They confirm that the Vadar-Morava Valleys and the many valleys and passes which open out from them were a major route for movements northwards and southwards.

Another more westerly route through the mountains is suggested by finds from the Bitolsko Polje area, for a number of sites, including Grgur Tumba and Porodin, point to independent connections with north-western Greece.

Fig. 12 Pottery from Starčevo (after Dimitrejević). c. 1 : 4

More distant connections, even at this early period, are suggested by the presence of obsidian fragments which came from the Carpathian Mountains and by the polished ornaments of stone (probably labrets or lip-plugs) which are best paralleled at Ali Kosh in Western Asia.[10] Another trade commodity is suggested by the cinnabar (red mercuric sulphide) found at Grabova, which probably came from Šuplja Stijena in Serbia.

Starčevo II, probably to be associated with the early fifth millennium, was distinguished by having painted pottery in some quantity. The phase was well-represented at Gornja Tusla where a subdivision was made on the basis of light designs painted on dark wares being followed by dark on light[11] but incised and applied-strip ornament was still common. The pot forms were now much more varied and included solid-footed cups but none of the vessels had handles of any kind. The designs on them were still arbitrary groups of straight lines and curves, although spirals had begun to appear.

Fig. 10

Other clay objects included figurines, now certainly female, loom-weights and spindle whorls. The forms can be paralleled in the Sesklo and Early Elateia Cultures of Greece and in the Veselinovo Culture of Bulgaria.

The last phase (III), which should belong to the later fifth millennium, besides being well-represented in Serbia, is found for the first time in the Drina Valley (at Obre near Kakanj) and in the Save Basin in northern Bosnia, and in eastern Croatia. The Starčevo site itself and the lower level at nearby Vinča seem to belong mainly to this phase.

The clay figures now had more realistically shaped bodies with protruding buttocks and the pottery more curvilinear patterns which included half-circles and circles. Of the vessels, more had incised and rusticated (pinched up) than painted ornament. There was also an increased use of bone, horn and antler for points and spatulas, and there were more clay spindle whorls and clay disc-stamps. Obsidian was now present in considerable amounts and flint-working still included the making of a few microliths. There are as yet no C14 dates for this phase, but those for similar material in Hungary are between 4500 and 4000 BC. This phase has many more similarities with the Körös complex in Hungary than have the earlier phases, and this might mean a movement of ideas or people from the north. If this was so, it was the first of a number of southward movements through Serbia and Bosnia in prehistoric and historic times.

Crvena Stijena Culture Whilst farmers of the Starčevo Culture were establishing themselves in the Middle Danube Basin other farmers were reaching the Adriatic coasts. Finds in Corfu, the Tremeti Islands and southern Italy show that pottery and ground-stone tools were in use in the southern Adriatic by the middle of the sixth millennium and recent work in Montenegro, Dalmatia and Hercegovina has recovered a whole series of sites with similar impressed and incised wares associated with groundstone tools.[12] There is no doubt that the new skills were reaching even the coast of Slovenia in this period. The finds have been named the Crvena Stijena Culture and in Dalmatia, at Smilčić, a large ditched enclosure with pottery, whose closest parallels were with the southern Italian impressed wares, has been found. Similar finds have also come from further north on the islands of Cres, Krk and Mali Lošinj, and on the coast in the Grotta della Gallerie near Trieste.

Penetration of the interior also took place; in the south in the Naretva Valley pottery similar to that of Crvena Stijena has been found at Zelena Pečina (level III) and at Novi Seher (level II), and in the north in the Postojna region of Slovenia.

Fig. 11

PERIOD II: THE SPREAD OF FARMING THROUGH NORTHERN
JUGOSLAVIA. MIDDLE NEOLITHIC PERIOD (*c.* 4500–4000 BC)

In the fifth millennium BC there was a steady development of farming
settlements in southern Jugoslavia and Dalmatia, and pioneers were
penetrating the mountainous areas of Bosnia, Croatia and Slovenia, so
that by the end of this period farming had become established throughout
Jugoslavia. Since there is little evidence of large-scale movements of
people from outside, the period is best seen as one of slow and largely local
development.

Vinča Culture In the Middle Danube Basin, some groups of the long-
established Starčevo Culture continued the changes noticed in Starčevo
III and spread along the southern margins of the Basin; these developments have been named the Vinča Culture. In the same way the
contemporary Linear-Ceramic Culture of the northern margins of the
Basin also developed, and both were impressive pioneering peoples.
Whilst the Linear-Ceramic Culture continued to seek loess soils like its
Starčevo-Körös ancestors and so spread farming through Central
Europe, the Vinča Culture turned to the valleys in hills and mountains
and so spread farming through central Jugoslavia. It may well be that
the patterns of 'transhumance' so well attested in later periods by Čerjel,
were already being established.

It is interesting that the Vinča, like the Linear-Ceramic Culture, is
not found in the plains of southern Hungary and northern Serbia where
the Starčevo-Körös Culture had its centre. From the first it was widespread in the hilly regions of the Lower Save, Drave and Morava Valleys,
and then extended over much of Bosnia and Hercegovina. It is also
interesting that it had many traits in common with the Linear-Ceramic
Culture. Both, for example, largely discarded the painted pottery
tradition and preferred dark-faced wares with incised ornament. It may
be that this preference which characterised much of Central and Eastern
Europe till Roman times was already present in Jugoslavia and shows
that its links were now closer with Central Europe than with the
Mediterranean world.

Vinča-Tordoš Culture The earlier phase of the Vinča Culture was also
found in the lower levels at Tordoš (or Turdas) in Romanian Transylvania, and is usually named Vinča-Tordoš. Because of good relative

39

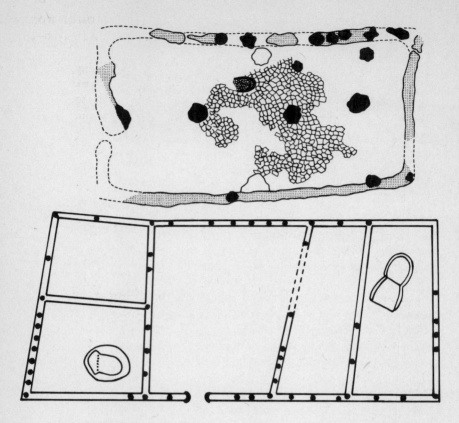

Plate 9

and absolute chronologies, this phase is well dated. At Vinča, for example, the three metres of rubbish which accumulated during this period underlay an equally long Late Neolithic occupation and from the Vinča-Tordoš level has come a C 14 date of 4240 ± 60 BC. Similar dates at Predonica and Fafos (4399 ± 150 BC) suggest that it began before 4000 BC and ended some five hundred years later.[13]

The general economy, like that of the Starčevo communities, was based on a mixed agriculture, in which breadwheat was increasingly grown and animals, particularly pigs, more commonly kept. This may have been because the deciduous forests were being exploited for fodder. Many of the settlements were on the same sites as before and 'tell' accumulations are found at Vinča, Crnokalačka Bara, Pavlovac and Porodin, and there is still no evidence of their being very large or

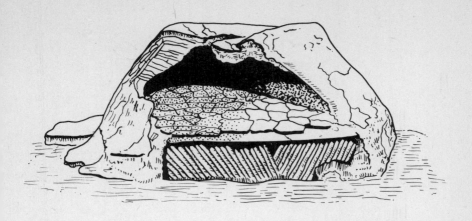

Figs. 13, 14 Plans of Vinča culture houses from Vinča and Banjica (after Garašanin, Todorović and Cermanović). c. 1:300
Fig. 15 Reconstruction of an oven from Vinča (after Vassić). c. 1:30

fortified. The accumulation of domestic debris suggests economies which allowed for permanent exploitation of the land round about, but on present-day ethnographic analogies this could have been done equally well by some form of shifting agriculture as by cropping or manuring cycles on continuously cultivated land.

The houses continued to be built in the old way of wood and clay, but although some larger ones are known they were not the immense 'long-houses' of the Linear-Ceramic folk. At Banjica, one without internal divisions measured about 12 × 6 metres, had its walls set in a foundation trench with postholes at irregular intervals and had large central post-holes which suggested a gabled roof. At Kormadin there were even plastered floors and walls with incised and applied ornament. Other house plans are known from the Matejski Brod and Pavlovac. Within the settlements well-made ovens, like those used in the region in recent times to make bread, were now common; models have come from Vinča and Valac (Kosovska Mitrovica). Whilst there is no evidence of any 'class' structure, this is not to say that it did not exist, since none of the villages have yet been completely excavated.[14]

Something of the religious beliefs of the people can be suggested. Burials continued, in accordance with the Starčevo rite, to be contracted inhumation in shallow pits. A cemetery of more than twenty burials at

Figs. 13, 14

Fig. 15

Botos had jars, bowls and in one case a figurine, buried with the dead. A few scattered burials occur among, but not inside, the houses.

In this period an increasing number of exotic objects are found; Mediterranean mussel (*Spondylus gaederopus*) shell ornaments were more common and so were fragments of marble, obsidian and cinnabar. The latter, like those in the later Starčevo levels, probably came from Šuplja Stijena in Bosnia, and may have been used for eye-paint. The presence of these materials suggests long-distance contacts and the finding of Vinča-Tordoš material in the Niš and Žarkovo regions of Serbia and in Macedonia could mean that the old route through the Vadar Valley into Greece was being used for trade. It may be significant that in the levels of this phase at Tordoš, near a source of copper ore, there were fragments of copper and that the same metal was also present in the contemporary Photolivos II and Sesklo Cultures of north-eastern Greece, not far from the Vadar Valley.

Plates 10–12   *Priština Art Style*   The settlement sites have yielded a mass of clay and stone models of animals, birds, objects and people, over fifteen hundred coming from Vinča itself. Although usually broken and discarded, they are well made and belong to a very distinctive artistic tradition sometimes called the Priština Style. Srejovic has distinguished three phases in the development of the male, female and sexless human figurines.[15] The first continued the Starčevo tradition and lavished great care on the modelling of the head, especially on the large lenticular eyes. The bodies became more naturalistic and had incised patterns and perforations, but were still often busts or three-quarter-length figures mounted on tripod-stands. In the second phase there was a more free modelling, but the artists still held to the old conventions; in the third, mainly found in later (Vinča-Pločnik) groups, there was a 'Free Realistic' style.

The stone tools still included shoe-last adzes and small unperforated triangular axes and there was still much poorly flaked flint and obsidian, but no stone arrow-heads or microliths. Deer antler seems to have been more used than before and hammer-heads and hafts for stone axes are found.

The pottery of this phase as distinguished by D. Garašanin carried on many Starčevo traditions, particularly those of its non-painted types, but had a wider repertoire of decoration and form. Plain dark burnished ware was most common but pattern-burnishing and incised ribbon and meander designs filled with rough dots are found. These incised styles resemble the contemporary Linear-Ceramic wares in Hungary. The pot forms included carinated and vertically-sided bowls, three- and four-footed pedestal bowls, tables (often called altars) with hollow feet, and rare lids and pots ornamented with animal faces; miniature forms were also made. Many of these pot-shapes are related to the Vesselinovo Culture of Bulgaria.

Plate 13

The distribution of the sites of this culture shows that it spread further to the south and west than its predecessor and its appearance in northern Bosnia and in eastern Croatia where it began to pioneer new climate zones is especially interesting.

It can be seen from this summary that the Vinča-Tordoš Culture was derived from earlier Middle Danubian traditions and was closely linked with contemporary Hungarian and Bulgarian cultures. There is nothing to confirm that it was due to immigrant peoples from further south, although it had far-reaching connections.[16]

Bitolj Culture   The Bitolj Culture, a contemporary group in the Lake Ohrid region of Jugoslav Macedonia, maintained its painted pottery tradition. At Bitolj there was, with Starčevo forms and ornament, painted pottery of Greek Middle Neolithic (Sesklo Culture) type. Obsidian and spatulas were in use, as they were further north.

Danilo Culture   In the Dalmatian coastlands and islands, as far north as Istria, there were new communities with painted pottery at this time. The earliest, known as the Danilo Culture, has better parallels in southern Italy and western Greece than in the interior of Jugoslavia, and was a sea-borne development, possibly brought by an immigrant people. The first phase of the culture, as distinguished by Korošec,[17] had, especially in the decorative use of interlocking meanders and the spirals with squared corners, similarities with the Ripoli and Square-mouthed Pottery Cultures in Italy and the Serra d'Alto Culture in the Lipari Islands. These belong to the later fifth millennium, so that the Dalmatian painted wares might well be contemporary with some of the impressed ware cultures already mentioned. The later phases at Danilo have parallels with the Drachmani and Elateia Cultures in Greece (4000–3500 BC), so that the culture has a long life.

The low tell formation of the settlement at Danilo Gornje on the Central Dalmatian lowlands suggests a considerable period of occupation and, if the shallow pits found really belong to huts, there were some 24 small houses partially paved with stones. No remains of plants or bones are reported but the plentiful stone industry included shoe-last adzes, small triangular axes and, a most interesting new development, a few barbed and tanged arrow-heads. Only eight pieces of obsidian were found. The pottery was of two main types, neither deriving from the Dalmatian impressed wares. One comprised the painted wares, a series of handled, bluntly carinated cups and pedestalled bowls with rim lugs, ornamented sometimes over a white slip, with broad bands or panels of red edged with black and filled with geometric patterns. The other consisted of plain burnished and incised wares with patterns of spirals, dots and meanders. The patterns were sometimes infilled with red paste. Clay stamp-seals and clay models, many of animal heads, were found.

Fig. 16

The distribution of this kind of pottery was very wide; in the north sherds come from the Trieste region and in the south from the island of Hvar, whilst others have also been found far inland at Zelena Pečina, Kakanj and Postojna.

By about 4000 BC, therefore, the spread of the new ideas had encompassed Jugoslavia and only in the mountain ranges and especially Slovenia is there as yet no evidence of farming.

PERIOD III: THE CONSOLIDATION OF REGIONAL CULTURES
AND THE BEGINNINGS OF METAL-USING (*c.* 4000–3500 BC)

During the fourth millennium BC the spread of farming through the whole country was completed. Some specialist, perhaps merely seasonal, pastoral settlements may be recognisable but there is nowhere any sign of surviving hunter/gatherer societies. It may well be that the many new regional cultures incorporated them.

There are indications that the first large-scale use of pure copper for heavy tools and weapons began at this time and that the local ores of the Middle Danube Basin were being exploited. Schubert[18] has shown that the greatest concentration of the shaft-hole axe-adze, the most typical tool, is in Hungary where the Bodrogkersztur Culture used local ores. Similar forms were used in the Vinča Culture area wherein lay the rich copper deposits of the Bor region.

Older theories have attributed the development of the European metal deposits to prospectors and traders from the Aegean, but on present

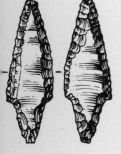

Fig. 16   Tanged arrow-head from Danilo (after Korošec). c. 1 : 2

evidence the European Copper (Chalcolithic) Age seems to have begun a thousand years before the Aegean trading networks, as known at present, came into existence. Unless there is some general error in the C14 dates for this period, metal-using is so early in the Balkans that it was contemporary with the 'pre-Troy' phase in Anatolia. In Jugoslavia, however, it is still difficult to find stratified evidence and many of the suggestions are based on the evidence from neighbouring countries.

Later Vinča (Pločnik) Culture   On the southern margins of the now long-settled Middle Danube Basin, the developed Vinča Culture continues. This phase is named Vinča-Pločnik after Pločnik, a typical Serbian site of the period.

Although some seventy sites are known, the culture is no longer found in many parts of northern Serbia where there had been numerous Vinča-Tordoš settlements. Instead it had spread southwestwards deep into Bosnia to become a culture of the hills and valleys rather than of the plains.

The chronology of this phase is established by both relative and absolute dating. At several sites it is stratified below Baden-Pecel Culture levels (*c.* 3000–2000 BC) (see p. 55) and, at others, above Vinča-Tordoš levels. This bracket is confirmed by absolute (C14) dates of 3895 ± 160 and 4070 ± 160 at Vinča and 3797 ± 60 at Gornja Tusla. There are also satisfactory correlations with contemporary Bulgarian (Karanovo IV-V) and Hungarian (Linear-Ceramic III-V) cultures.

In its economy, the mixed agriculture of the previous phase continues with little change and the long-occupied settlements like Hrtkoviči, Pločnik, Gradac and Priština (Kosovska Metohija) were still composed of rectangular, gabled houses of wood, clay and stone. The gables were still sometimes decorated, as at Jakova (Kormadin), and full-scale clay heads with real cow horns have been found. Clay ovens continued in common use.

Its material culture was also similar to the previous phase, although the triangular ground-stone axes were now occasionally supplemented by well-drilled shaft-hole axes and maces which parallel the copper ones mentioned below. Horn, shell and bone also continued to be used and cinnabar and obsidian to be imported. The appearance of copper objects, especially axe-adzes, is a sign of things to come. At Vinča, Gornja Tusla and other sites, copper hooks, usually described as fish-hooks (but equally likely to be belt-hooks), pins, beads (made from twisted strips) and lengths of plain strip have been found. These are simple to make and require only a limited knowledge of metallurgy. Before the end of the Vinča-Pločnik Culture more elaborate forms and even the alloying of metals were known. From Pločnik itself comes a hoard of thirteen copper chisels or narrow axes, a fine shaft-hole axe-hammer of Transylvanian form and two stone adzes.[3] The effect of the metal on everyday life is uncertain, for other aspects of the Vinča-Pločnik Culture continued with little change.

The recognition of the phase rests largely on the pottery.[18] Although many Vinča-Tordoš forms survive, taller and more carinated shapes are popular and strainers and four-legged vases, tables and anthropomorphic lids appear. There are still few true handles. Grey and black slips and fabrics are more common and are combined with combed, stamped and simple incised designs on the inside as well as the outside of the rims and necks. The incisions are often infilled with white paste. A subdivision of the phase has been seen in the appearance in the upper levels of several sites of painted ornament applied before or after firing.

Plate 14 Human figurines continue to be made, in Srejović's 'Free Realistic' phase of the Priština style, and some are now more than 50 cm. high. They are now most skilfully executed and the treatment is highly sophisticated. Females predominate and include crouched, seated (throned is perhaps too speculative a description), and baby-carrying figures. Many have incised patterns which suggest clothing and orna-ments, are encrusted with red or white paint after firing and have head, body and leg perforations. The heads are still modelled with great care, and have stylised faces, the noses and eyes being particularly prominent. Good examples come from Predonica and Aleksandrovac.[20] The finding of groups of these figures at Divostin (Kraguejovac) and Smederevska Palanka with tripod cups suggests they had a religious purpose, and the large numbers found at Vinča and Gradac, that they were produced in specialist workshops.

The reduction in area of this culture seems to have been due to the expansion of two neighbouring ones. In the Banat there was an en-croachment by the Tiszapolgar-Bodrogkeresztur Cultures along the Tisza Valley and in southern Serbia the Salcutsa Culture spread west-ward along the Nišava Valley.

On present evidence the rich Bosnian and Croatian valleys to the north and west of the Vinča-Pločnik farmers were thinly occupied at this time, for only from the Save and Bosna Valleys are sites known, and they have connections with the Lengyel and late Linear-Ceramic Cultures of Hungary as well as with the Vinča-Počnik Culture of Serbia. It is interesting to speculate on the importance of 'transhumance', the seasonal movement of livestock to and from pastures in the mountains at this period, for on the evidence of later times it might well have determined the way in which Bosnia and Croatia were developed.

Babska-Lengyel Culture   The Babska and Vučedol (layer X) settlements had flat-bottomed red and grey wares with lugs often lengthened to points or arranged in vertical lines, and these, especially when found on asymmetrical bottles, are of Lengyel type. Other forms, especially bowls, have elaborate incised ornament of late Linear-Ceramic style and applied cordons with fingertip impressions. Bone as well as stone shaft-hole axes and mace-heads (again similar to those at Lengyel sites) were found and much flaked flint-work, including barbed and tanged arrow-heads. Sites like Samatovici and Jakova (Kormadin) have Vinča-Pločnik traits including pottery with incised ornament, shoe-last adzes and figurines perforated in the hips, shoulders and head. In Bosnia, but still in the Save Valley, similar settlements of farmers have been found at Donja Mahala and Donja Klakar. They had flat and shoe-last adzes, barbed and tanged arrow-heads, microlithic industries which might show the influence of local hunter/gatherers, and pottery of Vinča-Pločnik forms on which is incised geometric ornament. The name Sopot-Lengyel culture has been given to the northern sites by Dimitrejević.[20]

Kakanj Culture   Farther to the southwest, but still in the Bosna Valley at Kakanj, Arnautovici and Mujevinia, similar groups carried forward this pioneering farming into a new and difficult environment. Saddle-querns, ground-stone axes, loom-weights and pottery which now often has applied cordon or marked horizontal zones of ornament, show that they took with them a mixed lowland Vinča/Lengyel inheritance. This complex has been named the Kakanj Culture and fragments of Danilo pottery, including a rhyton, show that it had connections with and owed something to the Adriatic coastal Neolithic Cultures.

Butmir Culture   When the Upper Bosna Valley, near Sarajevo, was

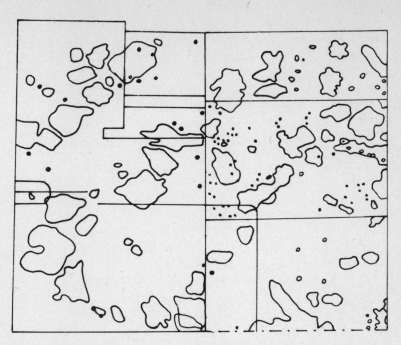

Fig. 17   Plan of part of the settlement at Butmir, showing pits and post holes. Excavated area 10 m. across (after Radimsky)

Fig. 18   Fine pottery from Butmir (after Radimsky). c. 1 : 4

reached, the nature of some of the material is sufficiently different for a new complex, the Butmir Culture, to be recognised.[21] This can be seen in part as a development from Vinča-Pločnik origins but there is much which is different and could have come from other sources in Dalmatia. The undefended and long-occupied settlement of Butmir was inhabited by efficient farmers growing, as in the Middle Danube Basin, bread-wheat, lentils and hulled six-row barley, and keeping cattle, sheep, goats and pigs. Apples, pears and hazel nuts were also found. Since there were few wild animal bones there was apparently little hunting, although disc mace-heads and barbed and tanged arrow-heads were found.

Numbers of irregular hollows and postholes in the settlement, and the finding of wattle-marked clay wall fragments, suggest houses like the earlier Middle Danubian and Danilo ones. The ground-stone tools included shoe-last adzes, flat axes and shaft-hole axe-hammers; much flint was also flaked and blade tools made.

Fig. 17

The finer pottery had undulating, spiral and concentric circle designs often infilled with hatching or dots and encrusted with red or white paste; some resemble Vinča-Pločnik, Danilo and Linear-Ceramic styles. The forms, especially the four-footed tables and the pedestalled bowls and vases, also suggest the Middle Danube Basin. The coarse pottery, however, which is naturally more common, is often chaff-tempered, ornamented with applied cordons and fingertip impressions.

Fig. 18
Plate 15

Other clay objects included conical loom-weights and human figurines. Many of the latter were female with dotted designs round the breasts or over the whole body and some were skirted. The heads were, as in the Vinča-Pločnik Culture, carefully moulded with elaborate hair-styles or hats.

Fig. 19 Pottery from Lisičići. c. 1 : 4

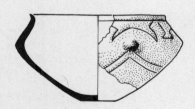

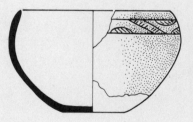

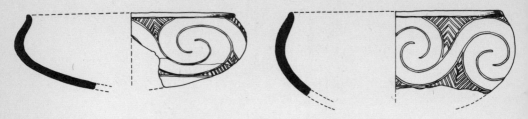

Figs. 20, 21   Above, bowls from Danilo; right, pottery rhyta from Danilo. c. 1:6 (after Korošec)

Even further west settlements and encampments of this period have been found. In the Bila Valley at Nebo (Travnik) a settlement of swineherds and hunters suggests either a seasonal camp or a specialised group within the economy of the mountain valleys.[22] The five depres-sions, four rectangular and one oval, which might be temporary huts, contained tools, pottery and figurines that linked it with Butmir. The animal bones were almost exclusively of pig and deer. At Lisičići, in a Hercegovinian valley leading to the Adriatic coast, similar encamp-ments of swineherds have been found with barbed and tanged arrow-heads and shoe-last and shaft-hole axes which seem to link them with Butmir and the interior of Jugoslavia. The encampment was of six huts, if the rather shapeless hollows can be interpreted in this way. Deer-hunting seems to have provided much of the food. The coarse pottery, comprising mainly handleless concave-sided bowls, was burnished and ornamented with incisions infilled after firing with red paste and suggests the Danilo Culture of Dalmatia (p. 43). A later group of the same people built a more substantial rectangular house here.

Later Danilo Culture It is now time to consider the Dalmatian coastlands, for whilst Vinča-Pločnik pioneers were penetrating Bosnia and Hercegovina from the east, there is evidence of increased settlement along, and inland from, the coasts. In North Dalmatia the later phases (II and III) of the Danilo Culture are found. At Danilo Gornje itself, besides incised and encrusted wares, there were sherds with cord impressions and barbed and tanged arrow-heads which probably show Central European influences (p. 52). Other exotic forms, like the four-legged animal-shaped vessels, are paralleled in Greece at Drachmani, Corinth and Elateia in the period 4000–3500 BC.[23] The penetration of these groups into Hercegovina and Bosnia has already been suggested.

Vlaško Culture In the Trieste region a northern variant of this culture

Fig. 19

Fig. 20

Fig. 21

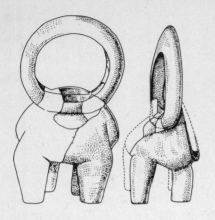

has recently been distinguished. Named the Vlaško Culture, it appears to be a development from local Mesolithic groups (p. 29). In caves like Ciclami, della Gallerie and Azzurra, typical late Danilo pottery, clay stamps and fine, barbed and tanged arrow-heads have been found with distinctive flint industries.[24]

Hvar Culture Further south a new culture – the Hvar Culture – is now found in Central Dalmatia on the island of Hvar, in the basin of the River Naretva in Hercegovina and even in the Poštojna region in Slovenia. On the island, the caves of Pokrovenik and Grabak were probably used by shepherds and goatherds and since no villages have yet been excavated the full economy is not clear.[25] Shellfish, including the mussel (*Spondylus gaederopus*) popular for ornaments in the Middle Danube Basin, were collected in large numbers. The deep cave deposits showed the culture to be long-lived and since incised pottery was common at all levels, especially in the middle phase, it is unclear how much of this culture was merely a development of the older Crvena Stijena Culture.[26]

The painted wares which distinguish the Hvar Culture have been divided by Novak into five successive phases. The older (I-II) were dark red with scroll and spiral patterns and had their best parallels in phase 3B of the Greek late neolithic Dimini Culture; they were also contemporary with the latest phase of the Danilo Culture. The younger (IV-V) were white slipped red ornamented wares, which were also found in the Tremiti Islands and resemble the Early Apennine Culture pottery from Italy, especially that from Grotta della Scalova. On the

Jugoslav mainland a variant of this culture has been recognised in Croatia, Hercegovina and Montenegro where at Zelena Pecina and Vršnik, it overlay Crvena Stijena Culture levels. A few objects of copper (p. 61) were found at Pokrovenik, showing, as on the Vinča-Pločnik sites, that a knowledge of metal came during this cultural period.

Northern Jugoslavia

It would seem from the scanty evidence that northern Jugoslavia (Slovenia and most of northern Croatia) lay outside the regions reached by the Starčevo and Vinča Cultures and was also unaffected by the Linear-Ceramic Culture. The earliest farming groups here owed much of their knowledge to the Central European Lengyel, Rössen and Mondsee Cultures. Sherds of the Danilo and Hvar Cultures in the Postojna region show that there was some penetration inland from the Dalmatian coast, but the finds at Drulovka, Ptuj and Kiringrad have their best parallels further north in Austria and Czechoslovakia.[26] The biconic flat-bottomed jars have channelled, comb- and cord-impressed ornament and the flint-work included microliths and fine barbed and tanged arrow-heads; socketed ladles also occur. The sites are not likely to have been occupied much earlier than 3000 BC. Occasional sherds of the distinctively incised Hungarian Bükk Culture, supposedly found at Vlaško Jama, Jama Kod Kolom and Jama Redjamskin, or comb- ornamented and cord-ornamented in Rössen Culture style from Vlaško Jama and Danilo Gornje also suggest influence from Central Europe.

Ljubljansko Barje Culture   The earliest of a group of sites in the marshes south of Ljubljana in Slovenia probably date from this time. They have been named the Ljubljansko Barje Culture, have been described as an Alpine facies of the Lengyel Culture, and had many connections with the Mondsee region of Austria.[27] As in Austria, lake-side sites were preferred and remained inhabited for many centuries. Some were over- whelmed by rising water and marsh and today lie below several metres of peat and mud so that much organic matter is preserved. The sites offer the earliest and most complete picture of Slovene farmers.

At Resnikov Kanal near Ig, the earliest finds were from a settlement supported by piles, and included ground-stone axes, wooden artifacts and dark-faced pottery. At Ajdovsko Jama there were comb-impressed pottery, some of it red-slipped, fine stone axes, some with shaft-hole perforations, antler tools and handles, and flaked bifacial points, some of them tanged. Parallels have been drawn with finds at Krško, Jermanova Jama and even Ptuj.

Other sites seem to be contemporary on the Karst plateau in the Trieste region, but only three have been noted by Barfield in northern Istria. At Zaule remains were well-stratified beneath 3 metres of alluvium, and probably represent a Vlaško type site with Vučedol parallels. Unlike any other part of Jugoslavia the connections are closest with eastern Italy. The obsidian from Vlaško Jama is of southern Italian origin.[28]

Southern Jugoslavia

In the extreme south, in the Morava Valley, the most obvious route between the Middle Danube and the Aegean, the Bubanj Hum Culture of the Niš region was contemporary with these developments and contained both Vinča-Pločnik and Greek Late Neolithic traits.

Bubanj Hum Culture   At Bubanj Hum itself in level Ia, red ware with white and black painted ornament, stone vases and ground-stone axes were found. This complex has the best claim to be Childe's Vadar-Morava Culture which was linked by him with some of the innovations found in Greece in the Late Neolithic period.[29]

CHAPTER III

The Earlier Bronze-using Communities

Fig. 22

Whilst stone- and copper-using farmers and pastoralists were exploiting the mountains and plains of Jugoslavia, bronze and gold were coming into use further to the south in Greece and Bulgaria, and to the east in Romania and Hungary.[1] The first bronze objects in Jugoslavia occur therefore in the later Neolithic-Chalcolithic cultures, especially in the most southerly ones of Vinča-Pločnik, Hvar and Bubanj. They may have owed their location to several different developments, for the Vinča-Pločnik Culture, as has already been shown, had links eastwards with Bulgaria and Romania, the Bubanj also with Bulgaria and southwards with eastern Greece, and the Hvar with southern Italy and western Greece. Opinions differ as to the length of the period during which a knowledge of metal-using spread through the Central Balkans and the nature of the process.[2] Most theories, based upon Anatolian and Aegean bronze and pottery typologies, postulate a spread from western Asia in the third millennium and see sophisticated urban communities like Troy and Byblos playing some part in it. There is no doubt that the development of metallurgy in the Balkans followed a very different and less sophisticated course from that in western Asia and the Aegean. In Jugoslavia, in particular, development was very slow; bronze did not come into common use until about 2000 BC and even then for several hundred years was restricted to a simple range of forms.[3] This delay may have been caused by the nature of the peoples of many regions by and to whom the knowledge of metal was spread.

It would seem that in the late fourth, third and earlier second millennium, ideas and perhaps groups of people were moving into Jugoslavia mainly from the east, for two important contemporary metal-using groups further north and south had little influence there although they certainly had on other neighbouring regions. In the south the Cretan and Greek cultures, Minoan and Helladic respectively, do not seem to have affected Jugoslavia until well into the second millennium, and in the north the Czechoslovakian and Hungarian Bell-Beaker Culture does not seem to have had any direct influence.[4]

It is also surprising how little contact there was with other contemporary and neighbouring groups to the north and west; cultures using cord-ornamented pottery and stone battle-axes were widespread in Hungary, Czechoslovakia and Austria but their influence on Jugoslavia was limited, whilst from Italy the influence was also very restricted.

The development of bronze-using in Jugoslavia may be traced through three stages: I (c. 2800–2300 BC) during which bronze-using spread; II (2300–1800 BC) during which new bronze and gold types are found; and III (1800–1450 BC when bronze was more common. A subdivision into IIIa and b at about 1650 BC, when more external influence was felt, is possible.

If factors other than metal-using are taken into account, the significance of these divisions is reduced. In Stages or Periods I and II metal was of very limited importance and stone was still the main material used. The spread of the Baden-Pecel Culture, its derivatives and parallel local developments were the most important events and do not seem to owe much to a knowledge of metal. It is only in Period III that metal plays an important part in everyday life. Even at this time it is found in a variety of localised cultures among whom there is no other unifying factor.[5]

Whilst attempts to correlate evidence of material culture and languages are to be treated with great caution, it must be mentioned that if, as some students of linguistics suggest, speakers of Aryan (Indo-European) languages entered Central Europe from further east during the Neolithic or Early Bronze Age, then the Baden-Pecel peoples have a better claim than most to represent some of them.[6] However, Burrow and others suggest that the Indo-European languages are native to Europe and that there is no archaeological evidence of mass migration from further east.

PERIOD I (c. 2800–2300 BC)

As already mentioned this period may be defined by the spread of the Baden-Pecel Culture and the development of local groups with similar traits.

Baden-Pecel Culture   The name Baden-Pecel has been given to a number of rather heterogeneous groups found in the Hungarian plains in the late fourth and early third millennium BC. In the latter millennium their distinctive pottery and equipment are found far to the north, west and south of Hungary unifying the areas previously covered by the Lengyel,

Fig. 22 Sites of the Early Metal Age in Jugoslavia

1 Ajdovsko Jama
2 Alihodže
3 Belegiš
4 Belotić
5 Bela Crkva
6 Bijelo Brdo
7 Blatno Brezovica
8 Bubanj Hum
9 Bezdanjača
10 Čot
11 Crvena Stijena
12 Deblak
13 Debelo Brdo
14 Donja Mahala
15 Donja Slatina
16 Dubanovci
17 Fafos
18 Gladnica
19 Glasinac; Kovačev Do
20 Gomolava
21 Gornja Tuzla
22 Gradac
23 Grapčevo Spilja
24 Hisar

25 Hocker (Pula)
26 Hrustovača Pećina
27 Humska Čuka
28 Ig
29 Ilandža
30 Jakova
31 Korbovo
32 Kostolac
33 Kličevac
34 Korićane
35 Krško
36 Lisičiće
37 Lasinja
38 Mokrin
39 Notranje Gorice
40 Omoljica
41 Pančevo
42 Prapatnica
43 Pelez
44 Pivnica
45 Pločnik
46 Predil
47 Prilep

48 Progar
49 Samograd
50 Savaš
51 Split (Gripe)
52 Srbski Krstur
53 Štinjan
54 Surčin
55 Škocjan (Toninčeva)
56 Tešanj
57 Varvara
58 Vattina
59 Velike Vrbica
60 Velike Gaj
61 Vinkovči
62 Vinomer
63 Vlaško Jama
64 Vrlazije
65 Vučedol
66 Zaule
67 Zelina Pećina
68 Zecovi
69 Zemun
70 Grotta del Muschio

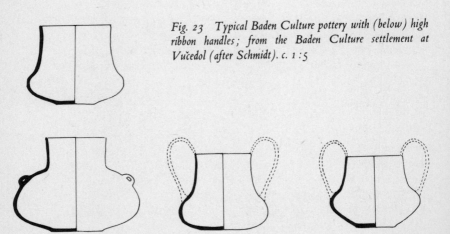

Fig. 23 Typical Baden Culture pottery with (below) high ribbon handles; from the Baden Culture settlement at Vučedol (after Schmidt). c. 1 : 5

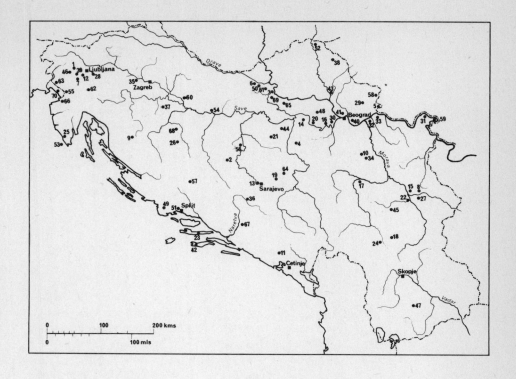

Vinča and Bodrogkeresztur Cultures. In Jugoslavia they used triangular
flint arrow-heads, shaft-hole axes, which can legitimately be called
battle-axes, and their pottery cups and jugs with channelled ornament
had strap-handles rising high above the rim. Horses and four-wheeled
carts, which seem to have a south Russian origin, were in use amongst
them and they had a knowledge of copper and bronze technology.
Sheep, cattle and pig bones are common in their settlements and this,
coupled with the abandonment of some of the settlements of other
cultures, the extensive use in Bosnia of 'gradina' or hill-top sites, and the
wide and relatively quick dispersal of Baden-Pecel types has led to
suggestions, perhaps over-confident ones, of their being a war-like
nomadic people.

Plate 16
Fig. 23

They appear in Jugoslavia along a wide front in the Lower Save,
Drave and Danube Valleys soon after 3000 BC. Their appearance
coincides with the end of many Vinča-Pločnik settlements.

Fig. 24 Reconstruction of the Baden Culture settlement at Vučedol (after Vičić and Schmidt)

At first the similarities between the Jugoslav and Hungarian sites are very strong, amounting at sites like Vučedol and Gomoblava to virtual identity. At these two sites several successive settlements of Baden-Pecel and derived cultures were found. At Vučedol, on a bluff above the River Save, the two-roomed apsidal-ended wooden houses were complete with hearths and saddle-querns, and had in and around them the characteristic pottery with high ribbon handles and channelled ornament reminiscent of metal forms, and copper and stone tools.[7] Similar material came from sites like Dubanovci and Perlez and even much further south (in level Ib) at Bubanj Hum. This seems to indicate a fast penetration of Jugoslavia along the main river valleys from the northeast to the southwest.[8]

The occupation was to be a permanent one, for in eastern Jugoslavia it has become possible to distinguish two groups which derive from the Baden-Pecel Culture.

Baden-Kostolac Culture   In central Serbia, the Save Valley and northern Bosnia, more than forty sites of the Baden-Kostolac Culture are known.[9] This culture was to have a long life and to have connections with the Cotofeni group in Romania and the Macedonian Early Bronze Age. Its metal types in particular show connections with Romanian Tran-sylvania. At Gomolava rectangular houses lay above Baden-Pecel ones

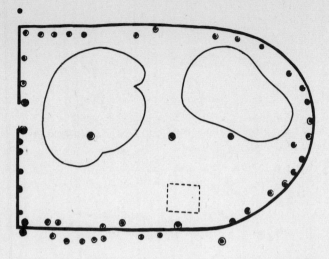

Fig. 25   *Plans of wooden houses in the settlement at Vučedol; the circles show hollows. Length of larger house 10m. (after Schmidt)*

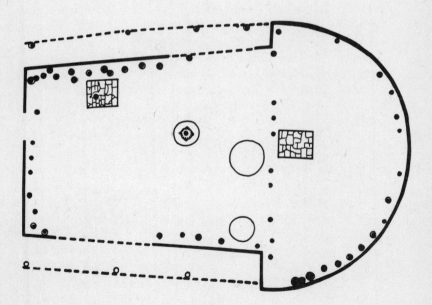

Fig. 26

and similar, 10 m. long, houses at Vučedol have been claimed by Tasić as belonging to this horizon. The pottery includes most of the older Baden-Pecel forms, now often ornamented with incised or comb-impressed patterns in horizontal or vertical zones.[10] At other sites like Pivnice, Cot and Koricane the pottery included round-bottomed, strap-handled jars, pedestalled goblets and bowls with incised and white-encrusted ornament. The two-handled goblet is a particularly interesting form, being found from Anatolia to Hungary; at Gladnice,

Fig. 27

Fafos and Hissar (Suva Reka) it should date to the beginning of the second millennium.

The single inhumation burials found at Vučedol indicate that some of the settlers were, unlike Neolithic peoples in the region, small and brachycephalic (round-headed).

Baden-Lasinje Culture In northern Serbia and the Drave basin the Baden-Lasinja Culture is known from some twenty sites. It too, at sites like Lasinja and Vindija, has a succession which carries on from the Baden-Pecel settlements. It also has links with the late Neolithic Lengyel

Fig. 26   Vučedol Culture house plan, Vučedol (after Schmidt). c. 1 : 200

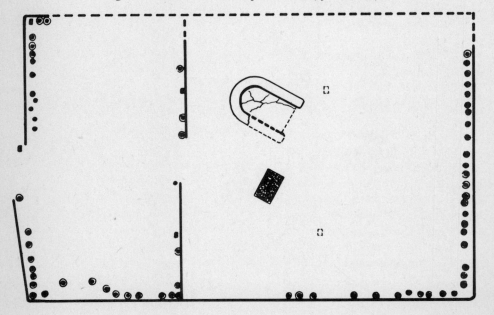

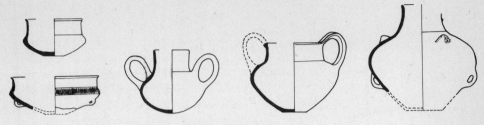

Fig. 27   *Pottery from Hissar, level 1a (after Garašanin)*

Culture for, as Dimitrijević has shown, the biconic pottery with strap-handles has its parallels at Lengyel. The metal objects included flat copper axes and, for the first time, moulds for them; needles; chisels; and from Progar a fine two-dimensional gold figurine, probably an import from Transylvania.[11]

In Serbia, at Humska Čuka, Jelenač and Kostov, painted rusticated and incised wares carry on earlier Neolithic traditions but rare strap-handles, lids and copper objects including a possible halberd are also found. In Bosnia and Hercegovina this influence spread down the river valleys, where it has been noted at Butmir and Lisčiće, and then on into Dalmatia, where it occurs in late Hvar Culture levels at Grapčevo Spilja and Zelina Pečina.[12]

Contemporary with these sites but rarely found on them, were copper shaft-hole axe-picks, axe-hammers, chisels and flat-axes of Transylvanian type. Widespread through Bosnia, Hercegovina and Croatia and often in hoards as at Tešanj and Kravido, they confirm that it was from the Middle Danube Basin that a knowledge of copper-using reached most parts of central and southern Jugoslavia. This probably took place well before 2000 BC.

Ljubljansko Barje Culture Further north, Baden-Pecel or Baden-Kostolac influence is less obvious, but copper is now found south of Ljubljana in the Ljubljansko Barje Culture.[13] At Ig-Studenec (phase I), beneath two metres of peat, five rectangular houses survive from this period. Their foundations were reinforced by piles and from them came evidence of mixed cereal (wheat and barley) and animal (cattle, sheep, pigs) farming, and of a variety of crafts. Here, as at Vinomer, bone and antler was much used for handles, and ceramic spindle whorls and loom-weights suggest spinning and weaving. The dark-faced pottery is

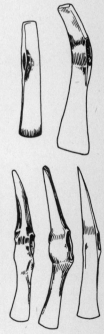

Fig. 28   *Copper axe-adzes and axe-hammers from Serbia. c. 1 : 4 (after Garašanin)*

Fig. 29   Stone shaft-hole axe-hammers from Vučedol. c. 1 :3 (after Schmidt)

ornamented with incised patterns often encrusted in white, and has lugs, and tunnel- or ribbon-handles. The shapes include many flat-bottomed, single-handled jars. There was much flaking and grinding of stone, and fine tanged arrow-heads and flat- and shaft-hole axes were made. A few flat-axes and one shaft-hole axe of copper were found. At Deblak under 3.3 metres of peat, dugout canoes made from large trunks 30 metres long probably belong to this period.

Similar pottery has been found in the caves of the Postojna and Trieste regions, especially at Vlaško Jama and Jama kod Kalom; these suggest a spread towards the coast. Its influence is best seen at Skočijan and Brivin.

The contemporary groups south of the Morava are little known. At Kosovska Metohija a probably independent group is represented. Hissar on the River Drim, which drains westwards into Albania, may have connections there. Further south sporadic finds from Macedonia, for example from Skopje, suggest connections with the Greek Macedonian Early Bronze Age.

PERIOD II (*c.* 2300–1800 BC)

Towards the end of the second millennium, perhaps after 2300 BC, new cultures were developing throughout much of Jugoslavia from the Lasinja, Kostolac and residual elements of the local late Neolithic cultures.

Slavonian or Vučedol Culture   In northern Croatia and Bosnia developed the Slavonian or Vučedol Culture which was to influence development over a wide area. Its origins lay in the Baden-Lasinja Culture, above which it was stratified at Vučedol, and it lasted until late in the first millennium.[14] It was one of a group of related cultures which succeeded Baden ones in the Middle Danube Basin. The settlements of rectangular houses are well illustrated by Vučedol. This culture showed a return to the appreciation of baked clay evidenced by the local Neolithic peoples. Besides the two-handled cups, elaborate four-footed pedestal bowls and tables, and three-legged bird-cups were made. These were ornamented by burnishing and by elaborate, excised dot and chequer patterns in horizontal zones, encrusted in white; their similarities to the present-day patterns for locally woven fabrics have often been noted. The same

Fig. 26

Plates 21, 22
Fig. 33

appreciation is shown in a great variety of clay figurines. These have sufficient traits in common for a Vučedol Style to recognized.

The Vučedol Art style The figures are usually three-dimensional, well modelled, burnished, and with incised and often white-filled detail. The presence of double axes, birds and, on the four-legged tables, of pairs of horns (the Horns of Consecration of Aegean archaeologists), has led to suggestions of religious connections with the Aegean.[15] Other figures, some of women in long skirts, others of animals, chairs and even pairs of boots or stockings very much like those worn today lack southern parallels and give some idea of the costume and equipment of the period. At Savaš and Vučedol itself particularly fine examples of these figures

Plate 23

Plate 16
Fig. 30

Fig. 30   Reconstruction of a woman's costume of the Slavonian-Vučedol culture (after Schmidt)

Fig. 31
Fig. 32

have been found. The burial customs still included single crouched inhumation and at Vučedol a deer was ceremonially buried. Stone shaft-hole axes, copper and bronze objects including a bracelet with incised ornament also belong to this phase.

Farther into the mountains of Bosnia, the cave of Hrustovača Pečina produced a variation of this culture with excised geometric patterns of well-made but apparently unencrusted red ware.[16] Less affected communities as at Donja Klakar and Donja Mahala still carried on the older traditions.

In Slovenia the still flourishing Ljubljansko Barje Culture is found through the period. At Notranje Gorica, a settlement which began in Late Neolithic times, cord-ornamented beaker sherds suggest connections with Czechoslovakia, whilst pedestalled bowls with incised crosses on the bases are best matched in the Rinaldone culture of northern Italy. A route between east Central Europe and northern Italy, especially through the Predil and Postojna passes, would seem to have existed.

The Ig Art Style Fine anthropomorphic vases and figures were now made in a distinctive art convention, the Ig Style, which owed something to the contemporary Slavonian-Vučedol Culture. Dark-faced, burnished and the incised features often encrusted in white, this ware

Plates 19, 20

included clothed figures and pairs of boots and perhaps trousers. Bone objects carved in the Vučedol style are also found.

On the coast, in Istria, near Trieste and on the plateau east of it, sites with sherds of this culture also occur. Barfield has shown that the corded-ware pottery found there has its best parallels in Austria and inland

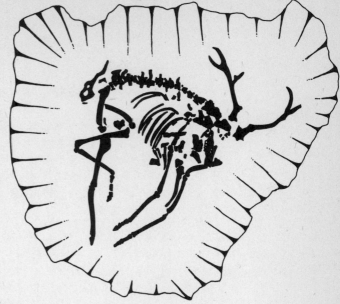

Fig. 31 Plan of a grave of the Vučedol culture. Width 3 m. (after Schmidt)

Fig. 32 Ceremonial burial of a deer, Vučedol. c. 1 : 17 (after Schmidt)

Fig. 33 Patterns on Slavonian-Vučedol pottery at Hrustovača Pećina (after Korošec)

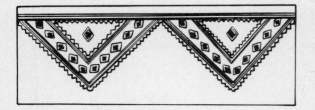

Slovenia,[17] and that it is the only certain evidence of Central European corded ware pottery related to Vučedol types reaching the Mediterranean. In Istria and Brijuni a separate Brijuni-Skočjan group has also been distinguished; its black burnished bowls with vertically pierced lugs likewise have eastern, Slovenian, connections and are found with Lagozza and Hvar Sherds. Copper objects from Skočjan, including a round-heeled dagger with rivet holes, and from Brijuni suggest that the group belongs to Period IIb.[18]

Bubanj Culture In southern Serbia and Macedonia the earlier phases of the Bubanj Culture are now found following the phase of Baden occupation. Sites on hill-tops like Bubanj Hum and Humska Čuka follow the pattern of the Salcutsa and Krivodol Cultures and have strong connections further east in Bulgaria and Romania;[20] for example at Ezero (Nova Zagora) and Yunatcite (Plovdiv). Shaft-hole and wedge-shaped copper axes, as at Prilep, now occur. Gradac, where a bronze pin was found with fine black burnished and grooved ware, should also belong to this period. Some evidence of connection with cultures to the north is suggested at Zok where Vučedol forms and white-encrusted ornament are found.

Hvar Culture In Dalmatia at this time the Hvar Culture seems to continue, for a Grapčevo Spilja a bronze bracelet was found with Hvar-type pottery. Hoards of copper shaft-hole axe-picks and flat axes, like those at Split Grippe are also found.

PERIOD III (1800–1450 BC)

Although the introduction of bronze-working is used by archaeologists to distinguish periods, the mere change to a new alloy of tin and copper, even though it be superior to pure copper, need not be accompanied by any great cultural upheavals. This is certainly true of Jugoslavia where the cultures already mentioned continued through the period in which bronze-using became common. The acceptance of bronze was slow and was not accompanied by the development of any strong local industry and there is no evidence that the rich ores of Bosnia or Slovenia were exploited until later.

The knowledge of the alloy probably came, like the new fashions in weapons and ornaments made from it, from two neighbouring regions of Central and Eastern Europe where strong bronze-using industries

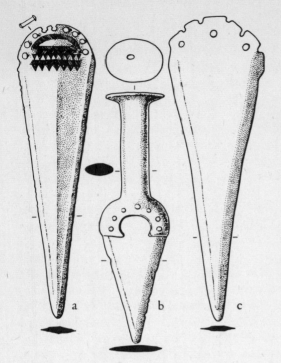

were established by 1800 BC. The influence of the Minoan and Mycenaean civilizations developing in the Aegean at this time, and affecting both Central Europe and Transylvania, seems not to have been felt until the end of the period and then only in the south and west.

    Since the rare metal, tin, must be added to copper to obtain bronze and the two are not often found together, the new industries must have required considerably more organisation than copper-working alone. Long-distance trade routes were certainly established, and hoards of metal objects suggest that smiths, as might be expected, recast worn-out pieces as well as introducing new supplies. Two-piece moulds mainly for weapons and ornaments are now found, and finishing and decorating are more elaborate. From Transylvania several single-edged forms of the long popular shaft-hole axe were adopted, and from Central Europe came the round-heeled rivetted dagger and varieties of flat and flanged axes. Ornaments for neck, ear, arm or leg were made of bronze or gold, taking the form of coiled wire or solid casting with incised patterns.

Fig. 34

The dating of the bronze objects and of the settlements in which they are found, rests both on comparison with finds from neighbouring countries and on well stratified sites. Subdivision of the period is possible at about 1650 BC, whereby the earlier phase IIIa (1800–1650) may be equated with the Early Unětice Culture of Central Europe (Gimbutas A) and the Early Helladic II – Middle Helladic I (2400–1900) in Greece; while Period IIIb (1650–1250) is contemporary with the Late Unětice (Gimbutas B) and the Middle Helladic II (1900–1750) Periods.

PERIOD IIIa (1800–1650 BC)

Before 1650 BC new metal fashions are found among some of the already established societies.

Slavonian-Vučedol Culture　In Croatia, the Slavonian-Vučedol Culture continued to spread its influence and develop its distinctive pottery styles which now owe something to contemporary Hungarian fashions.[21] The pottery at sites like Vinkovci has beautifully executed incised and stamped patterns, and bronze is present. A round-heeled dagger from Jakovo (Komadin), a mould for a flanged axe from Savaš, and a hoard of shaft-hole axes and a bronze flat axe from Becmen could also belong to this time. Single crouched inhumation was still being practised.

Ljubljansko Barje Culture　In Slovenia, the Ljubljansko Barje Culture continued to flourish and at Blatno Brezovica, beneath 2 metres of peat, a platform or causeway 7 metres wide and more than 20 metres long was reinforced by lines of piles. On it a rectangular hut with a wooden floor and two hearths was built. Wheat, especially breadwheat, barley and millet, were grown, reaped with flint sickle-blades and ground on saddle-querns; cattle and a few pigs and sheep were also kept. Here, as at Ig-Studenec (phase II), a wide variety of clay, wood, bone, antler and stone objects was found. It included shaft-hole stone axes of Central European type, fine flaked flint blades and much pottery. The latter showed a series of flat-bottomed jars and bowls with multiple lugs but little ornament which, according to Korošec, show influence from Croatia.[22]

Periam/Mokrin Culture　A very different culture is found at this time in northern Serbia, southern Hungary and western Romania. This, the Periam (or Perjamos) Culture, has, in its earliest phase in Hungary, many indications of Aegean connections, especially in its metal and pottery types and in its ornaments of faience (glazed frit) and mediter-ranean shell.[19] Its most southern province was in northern Serbia where the Mokrin Culture is now distinguished as a separate and southern facies of it. Although bronze is used, copper and knobbed stone shaft-hole battle-axes, like those in contemporary Central European Battle-Axe Cultures, are found. At Bela Crkva stone shaft-hole battle-axes, which copied metal ones, were found with a round-heeled three-rivet bronze dagger.

Bubanj Culture In southern Serbia the Bubanj Culture continues into a phase typified by two-handled globular vessels, and similarities with the famous Minyan ware (Middle Helladic I) of Greece are reported. It had much stronger connections eastwards with Romania and Bulgaria, where the Glina III Culture, which also used flanged axes, round-hilted daggers and shaft-hole axes, was developing.

All the cultures just discussed lie north and east of the mountains; in the mountains, from Montenegro to Croatia, there is little evidence of anything but local development. Some communities like those on the hill-top of Debelo Brdo and in the cave of Hrustovača Pečina carry on the Slavonian-Vučedol ceramic traditions; others, like those in the earliest levels at the long-occupied site of Zencovi and in the latest levels at Donja Klakar, seem to continue the local Late Neolithic traditions. At Debelo Brdo the settlement was partly strengthened and defended by piles and besides the white encrusted geometrically ornamented pottery, polygonal shaft-hole axes were found. Caves still seem to have been used, perhaps as in earlier times, by shepherds and swineherds, for besides Hrustovača Pecina, remains have been found at Crvena Stijena (Montenegro). At Zencovi, a hill-top site, there appeared in this period white encrusted Slavonian-Vučedol type pottery, applied cordon orna-ments, strap-handles and fragments of cast bronze.[22]

The influence of the Slavonian-Vučedol Culture also reached Dalmatia. On the island of Hvar in Grapčeva Spilja and at Zelina Pecina the pottery had traits of this culture.

Throughout this wide region, but usually apart from the settlements, a scatter of finds shows that new metal fashions were being adopted: flanged axes, as at Tiskovac and Tesanj, and rivetted daggers as at Hocker in Istria and Stijan on Brijuni Island.

Plate 24

Fig. 35

69

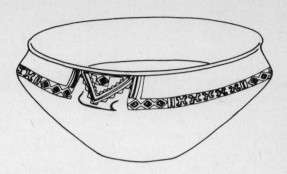

Fig. 35   Bowl from Zencovi, layer 5. 1 : 5 (after Benac)

PERIOD IIIb (*c.* 1650–1450 BC)

A division can be made at *c.* 1650 BC not only because of changes in the metal types and the growing influence from Mycenaean Greece, but because of the spread of the two complexes of burial rites previously favoured further north and east. These rites, which were to remain popular for a millennium cannot, from their associated finds, be seen as the result of invasions of large numbers of people. Instead, either a spread of religious ideas or of small and influential groups seems possible.

The burial of single bodies, often with elaborate rituals, beneath round barrows, was widespread in Europe in the second millennium BC. In Jugoslavia there is no evidence of it in Neolithic or Copper Age times but it was widely adopted in the Bronze Age, especially in the hills and mountains from Serbia to Slovenia. Since the inhumations were accompanied by the pottery of local cultures, the rite is best seen as having been adopted by a number of separate communities.

West Serbia Tumulus Culture   At present, the earliest recognizable groups are in east Bosnia and neighbouring western Serbia and have been called the West Serbia Tumulus Culture.[24] It is not possible at present to do more than see similarities to the Central European rites and they cannot be assumed to show a large-scale invasion from that region. In the Valjevo region of Serbia, especially at Belotić and Bela Crka, round mounds of earth cover small stone cairns and circular spreads of stones. The single crouched inhumations were accompanied by local (Bubanj Culture) pottery and rare bronze objects. At Belotić, Tumulus

X, these consisted of a round-hilted rivetted dagger, a ring-ornamented bracelet and an awl. In Bosnia in the Glasinac valley (Romanija), the mounds were raised over inhumation graves sometimes surrounded by stones and accompanied by stone battle-axes and round-hilted rivetted daggers.

Fig. 51

Glasinac Culture These are attributed by Benač and Čović to Period I/IIa of their Glasinac Culture.[25] Some of the sites, as at Kovacev Do and Vrlazje, also show northern connections in their metal objects. Although comparably early burial mounds in Croatia or nothern Serbia have not yet been found and the route to the south is therefore unclear, it is unlikely that the rite was invented in Bosnia and southern Serbia. It should probably be seen as an adoption from Central Europe whence there is good evidence for the rites spreading to many new regions at this time.

Another example of the spreading of these rites may be seen in Slovenia and western Croatia although no separate tumulus culture has yet been identified.[25] Brinjevo Gora in Slovenia may be as early as this period, and so may Hocker in Istria, where a tumulus covered a stone cist in which was a round-heeled rivetted dagger. These are much more likely to be linked directly with the Central European Tumulus (Developed Unětice) Cultures.

Fig. 46

Cremation as a burial rite is occasionally found in Europe, although not in Jugoslavia, from early Neolithic times onwards, and in the Middle Danube Basin in the Bronze Age it came increasingly into favour. After cremation, all or some of the ashes and bone fragments were collected from the pyre and buried. The variety of rites used might include placing the ashes and other objects in a pot (urn) and when a number of these urns found together the cemetery is called an urnfield.

Pancevo-Omoljica Culture These rites were beginning to be popular in the Banat and Vojvodina regions of northern Serbia in this (IIIb) period and from then on spread into many parts of Jugoslavia. The Pancevo-Omoljica Culture, ancestral to the Vattina Culture (p. 78) seems to be the earliest Jugoslav Urnfield group. At Pancevo itself a series of biconic urns, some with handles and most with channelled and curvilinear ornament often infilled with dots and encrusted with red or white paint were found. At Vattina a settlement site also apparently from this time has been uncovered.

Plates 27, 29

Metal objects, including flanged axes, a single-bladed shaft-hole axe, spiral lock- or ear-rings and bracelets, which from their shapes could belong to this period, also come from the Klicevac, Zuto Brdo and Bjelo Brdo urnfields and suggest that these cemeteries were beginning to be used (p. 80).

In regions where the new burial rites were not introduced, the adoption of new metal and pottery fashions from other communities distinguish this period. In northern Serbia the Mokrin-Periam Culture influence was strong and the gold objects from Velika Vrbica could well belong to it. The sophisticated gold beads, ivy-leaf pendants and ear-rings can be matched in Transylvania, whence no doubt the gold came. Omoljica (level 3 and 4), Illandze (level 1) and in northern Serbia, Belegiš (level 2 and 1) and Surčin should belong to this period. At Surčin metalwork included round-heeled rivetted daggers, chisels, flat axes and a Czech (Bohemian) type of flanged axe. The gold armband from Bilje also has its best parallels further to the north-east.

Paraćin and Slatina Cultures Further south in Serbia two other groups can be recognized. Connected with the Middle Danubian cultures of this period is the Paraćin Culture of the Lower Morava Basin. This is characterized by two-handled vessels of globular form. In the Upper Morava Basin a local development is known as the Slatina Culture. Settlements at Velika Humska Čuka and Donja Slatina (Leskovac) have pottery of which one of the characteristic new forms is a two-handled bowl with buttons on the top of the handles; this again is well paralleled in Bulgaria at Karanovo (level VII) and Sveti Kyrillovo. Other handles

Fig. 36   Vase with studs on the handle; Paraćin, grave 4

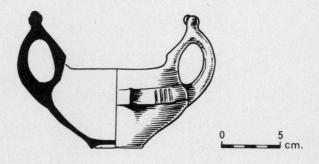

0   5
cm.

Plate 25

Fig. 36
Plate 27

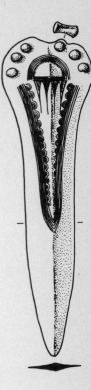

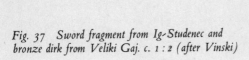

Fig. 37   Sword fragment from Ig-Studenec and bronze dirk from Veliki Gaj. c. 1 : 2 (after Vinski)

are held to resemble Middle Helladic Greek ones but in spite of much searching there has been no significant find of Minyan ware or forms in this region.[26] There are, however, biconic cups with cylindrical necks and channelling on the shoulders which are also found further north in Serbia.

In Slovenia, in the continuing Ljubljansko Barje Culture, there are now fine ogival daggers with incised ornament, moulds for shaft-hole axes, and from the river at Ljubljana, a flanged axe. Finds from the Drave Valley in northern Slovenia show that the routes into Central Europe were being used; that these continued to the Adriatic Sea is suggested by the evidence from Dalmatia, where a scatter of Central European bronze forms, like the fine metal-handled dagger from Patpatnica, was reaching the coast. There is no evidence of Aegean influence in Dalmatia then.

Figs. 34, 37

CHAPTER IV

The Climax of the Bronze Age

The seven hundred years or so before 700 BC was a period in which the tempo of change appears to have increased. The amount of archaeological evidence is much greater than before, probably because an increasing population was exploiting the country, helped by a steadily improving, but still bronze-dominated, metallurgy and perhaps by the formation of larger social units.

Events in Jugoslavia at this time must be seen in relation to the great drama being enacted a few hundred miles away; first the climax and collapse of Mycenaean, and then the slow rise of Classical Greek and Italian, civilizations. In both series of events Jugoslavia played some part and movements of peoples from the Middle Danube Basin into Greece and Italy can be seen. Within Jugoslavia these movements were probably responsible for the increasing popularity and intermixing of the 'tumulus' and 'urnfield' burial rites (p. 70) and for the fortification of a large number of sites. Before the end of the period some of the archaeologically-recognizable cultures can be tentatively linked with historically-known tribes whose languages were Illyrian (p. 99).

Although no single chronological scheme can be used for the whole of Jugoslavia for this period, the collapse of the Mycenaean kingdoms in the twelfth century BC was reflected in all the regions, and it is reasonable to make the division into the traditional Middle Bronze Age and Late Bronze Age at this point.

THE MIDDLE BRONZE AGE (*c*. 1450–1200 BC)

In this short period there were in fact three major phenomena; the indigenous metallurgical industry seems to develop quite suddenly; long-distance trade-routes which pass through the country from north to south are opened up; and the first of a new series of migrations from the Middle Danube Basin is evident. The first two may be seen as the direct effect of Aegean commercial expansion, but the third may well have been part of a 'backlash' which helped destroy Aegean Bronze Age civilization.

74

The period from *c.* 1450 to 1200 BC is most precisely defined by metal types, but since these are rarely limited to cultural groups defined by other criteria, changes in them should not be taken to indicate any change in the population unless accompanied by other evidence. The dating of the period can be fixed with some precision through the connections with the Minoan/Mycenaean civilizations, the Únětice Culture of Central Europe and the Otomani Culture of Hungary. It is unlikely to have begun earlier than Middle Helladic IIb in Greece (1850–1750) or full Únětice times (Gimbutas II, Reinecke IIb) and ends with the collapse of the Mycenaean kingdoms and the development of the Middle Danubian and Alpine Late Bronze Age industries about 1200 BC.[1]

Now for the first time over much of Jugoslavia the industry probably owed its growth to local development and to the exploitation of the Bosnian and Slovene ores.[2] It was no doubt greatly influenced by the increased contact with Mycenaean Greece and with the developed native industries in the Middle Danube Basin and in Central Europe.

Gold, as well as copper and tin, was now regularly in use, and the techniques for working these metals included casting in two- and three-piece moulds, casting-on, hammering and annealing. The finding of some hoards with tools and ingots suggests smiths, whilst others with large groups of finished pieces point to merchants.

Fig. 38

The majority of the metal objects were still weapons or ornaments. The weapons include rapiers and swords, which show a variety of influences at work. The round- or square-butted, narrow-bladed rapiers, which sometimes, as at Ig, have incised ornament, show Central European influences; others, as at Tetovo, have the horned guard of a well-known Mycenaean form. Wider-bladed swords, solid- or, by the

Fig. 39

Fig. 38 *Donja Dolina; moulds for Late Bronze Age objects (after Radimsky). c. 1 : 4*

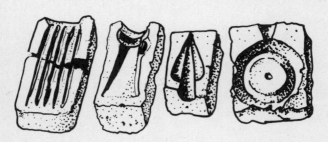

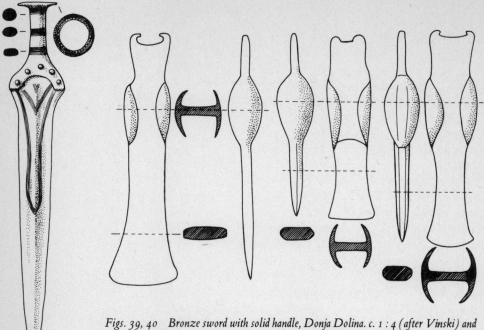

Figs. 39, 40   Bronze sword with solid handle, Donja Dolina. c. 1 : 4 (after Vinski) and a hoard of bronze medial-winged axes from Monte Maesta (after Gnirs)

end of the period, tongue-grip-hilted, as at Vattina and Sv. Kočjan, show Hungarian and Alpine influences. Shaft-hole battle-axes were also widely used; those with moulded shafts, stud terminals, long narrow or wide dropping blades are Middle Danubian, whilst the symmetrical double-axes are of Aegean styles. Palstaves and medial-winged axes, as at Štinjan are, like many of the socketed spears, Central European types. Possible fragments of Aegean-style body-armour made from split and perforated boars' tusks, and a stud from a cap-shaped helmet have also been found at Vattina.

The ornaments show a similar variety of fashions; pins are common, especially variations of the 'pershaft knot' pin, sometimes with a twisted shank, and pendants of ivy-leaf form as at Paraćin, Bijelo Brdo and Glasinac. These, like the use of gold, copper or bronze wire to make small lock-rings and large arm-rings, show Middle Danubian influence. Solid penannular bracelets with slight expanded terminals, as found as

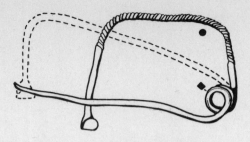

Fig. 41   Fibula from the hoard at Podnita. c. 7 : 8 (after Vinski-Gasparini)

Glasinac, reflect Central European fashions and by the end of the period a Central European invention, the 'safety-pin' type of brooch, is widespread. In the Pričac hoard, the crescent-shaped cheek-piece from a horse bridle, one of the earliest from the region, should be noted.[3]

Fig. 41

There is evidence at this time of the use of some routes over very long distances, perhaps as 'barter-chains' along which ideas and objects passed to and from Northern Europe and the Aegean world. Jugoslavia lay across or beside some of the most important of these routes.[4]

The sea route through the Adriatic is particularly well attested although, as in later times, the Italian coast was probably preferred to the Dalmatian. In Istria connections with the north Italian Terremare Culture are present, and suggestions of a direct connection with Mycenae have been made. Further south in the Zadar/Split region, objects with pulley and running spiral ornament, double axes like those from Kočevlje, the daggers and rapiers and the miniature ox-hide ingot from Makarska show that Aegean ideas were coming from the south, but no finds of Mycenaean pottery have yet been made in Dalmatia.

The tongue-grip sword from Sv. Skočjan, the trapeze-hilted dirk from Osor, the fibulae from Unesić show that ideas and objects were also arriving from the north, and amber is very likely to have reached Albania and north-western Greece by this route.[5]

A land route from northern Greece via the Morava Valley to the Transylvanian mines was also in use in this period.[6] Aegean influence shows in the pottery of the Slatina and Paraćin Cultures (p. 72), perhaps in the four-spoked wheel of the Dupljaja chariot and in metal objects like the Tetovo sword. Transylvanian and Hungarian influence also came south and west along the trade routes. It is found in Serbia and Bosnia in this period, for example in the spiral wire bracelets, shaft-hole

Fig. 48

Fig. 42   Reconstruction of the Dupljaja figure with umbrella. Height approx. 15 cms

Fig. 43   Grave group from Dobrača, tumulus VII, grave A. c. 1 : 4

axes and fish-scale ornament at Glasinac. Some of these types, especially the shaft-hole axes, reached northern Greece by this route.[7] The same influence was also widespread through Croatia and Bosnia-Hercegovina to the Adriatic coasts at this time, and continued to be strong into the Late Bronze Age.

Another land route, perhaps via the Save Valley, brought specifically Central European types to Bosnia; for example the violin-bow safety-pins (a better name, perhaps, than fibulae or brooches) found at Strbči (Tumulus I grave I) and Taline (Tumulus XIV grave I), and the flat-headed pin at Hrustovača Pečina.

Whilst many of the settlements of this period are on the same sites and attest the same ceramic traditions and burial customs as before, there is one area, the southern margins of the Middle Danube plain, which shows that both development and movements of peoples took place.

Vattina Culture   In the Banat and Vojvodina regions, the Vattina Culture can be seen as a development of the Pancevo groups who, as already described, cremated their dead. Over a wide area, in cemeteries like Korbovo (Oltenia), Vras, Banatska Polanka and Temes Kubin

Fig. 51

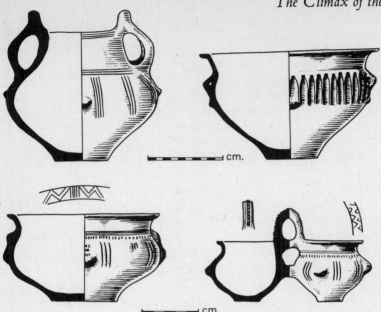

there are biconic, necked urns and bowls with the cremations. These are closely paralleled in the Girla Mare and Verbicioara Cultures of Romania, and Berciu and others have seen the whole area as forming a single cultural unit.[8] It is interesting that in Romania changes from inhumation to cremation also seem to have taken place unassociated with any large-scale population upheaval.

The economy of the culture was based on the same crops and animals as before, although the horse was more common and bone cheek-pieces from bridles are found. The considerable depth of deposit (up to two metres) suggests stable communities. The settlements contain, like the cemeteries, cylinder-necked pots, bowls, and double cups with grooved handles. They have curvilinear or cord-impressed ornament and, as a new development, fluting to give a 'turban' effect on rim or shoulder. There are a few clay figurines and phalli, stone shaft-hole axes and maces, and flaked flint and obsidian. The stone moulds for metal objects and the objects themselves are of Hungarian type. At Vattina, both Central and Southern European bronze forms were found and show that the culture had connections with distant regions.[9]

Plate 26

Plate 29

79

Dubovac-Kličevac Culture   Also in northern Serbia and neighbouring regions was the closely-related Dubovac-Kličevac Culture, from which cemeteries and settlements are also known. In the undefended settlements, as at Kličevac, there was much flaked flint and some obsidian; among the bronze objects, the battle-axes, spiral rings and bracelets showed Hungarian Bronze Age (Period IV – Koszider horizon) connections.[10]

Fig. 44

The Kličevac Art Style   Clay models of chariots, women, battle-axes and chairs were found and from them a distinctive Kličevac Art Style has been identified.[11] In the case of the human figures, which are fully three-dimensional, more attention was paid to the incised than to the modelled detail; the females wear long skirts, bodices and jewellery. The

Plate 28
Fig. 42

most interesting model, from Dupljaja, is a chariot drawn by three water-birds which probably had a canopy over the standing figure of a clothed and bejewelled female. Trbuhovic and others believe these figures to show Aegean inspiration but they can equally well be seen as continuing the ancient local artistic tradition.

The graves usually contained two-storeyed urns covered by one-handled dishes and hollow stands. The stamped and channelled curvilinear ornament, like that on the models, was often encrusted with red or white paste.

Bijelo Brdo Culture   A third related group is found farther west in Croatia and has been called the Bijelo Brdo Culture.[12] It has many parallels in its pottery shapes with those found farther east, although double pots are missing and the ornament tends to be a series of finely-drawn concentric half-circles and circles. In settlements and cemeteries like Surčin (phase I) and Belegiš (phase I), the metal sickles, pins and beads show Hungarian connections. From Surčin also comes a marble disc with a 'triskele' pattern of Aegean inspiration.

There is increasing evidence that in this period new movements of people from the Middle Danube lowlands began to take place. The direction, speed and distances covered in these movements suggest that the routes opened by trade were followed southwards, westwards and northwards by raiders and settlers. That these were actual movements of people and not merely of ideas is shown by the pottery, for at many well-stratified sites almost complete changes in domestic pottery traditions can be observed. Eastwards in Romania, the Girla Mare Culture was replaced before the end of the period by peoples using pottery of

Dubovac-Kličevac type.[13] Southwards in Bosnia, Slavonian-Vučedol
Culture settlements gave place to Middle Danubian 'Urnfield' ones at,
for example, the long-used hill-top settlement at Zencovi where level 3
contained the new fluted rims, and high-handled cup forms. At
Hrustovača Pečina, a violin-bow safety-pin of Central European origin
was found with the 'Urnfield' (Middle Danube) type pottery and similar
pottery came from level 2 at Crvena Stijena in Montenegro.[14] On some
of the more southerly sites the rites are mixed with those of the 'Tumulus'
cultures; for example at Dobrača, barrows covered cremations which
had with them pottery of Vattina Culture type.

Fig. 45

Fig. 43

Fig. 44   Clay figure in the Kličevac art style, from Kličevac (after Kossak)

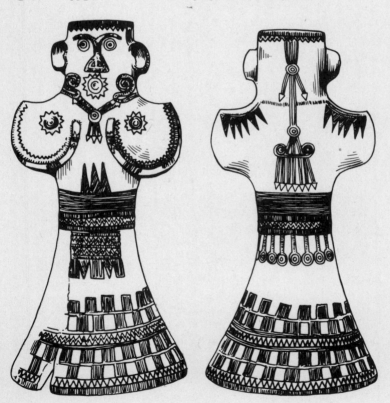

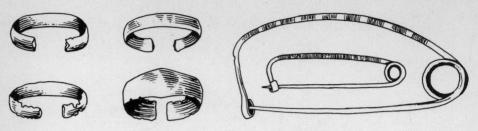

Fig. 45 A group of bronzes, including early stilted safety-pins, from Hrustovača Pećina (after Korošec). c. 1 : 3

There is good reason to suppose that the movement of these peoples continued southwards through Albania and Macedonia into Greece and the Aegean coastlands, and that they played a part in the destruction of Mycenaean Bronze Age civilisation.[15]

Movement to the northwest also took place. In Italy the earliest of a long series of 'Urnfield' cremation cemeteries date back to these times and Hencken's recent and detailed comparison of the pottery from them and from the Middle Danubian cemeteries shows a complex of traits com-

Plate 30

mon to both regions.[16] The Italian two-storeyed urns, one-handled dishes, double pots and the curvilinear-encrusted style of ornament were especially closely matched in the Vattina-Dubovac/Girla Mare complex. It is difficult not to see some of the Italian 'Urnfield' peoples as invaders from Jugoslavia.

During this same period the use of tumuli to cover inhumations continued in western Serbia, eastern Bosnia and even appears in other regions. In western Serbia, as already mentioned, cremated remains now began to be buried under tumuli sometimes with pottery of Vattina Culture type. The bulk of the pottery, which continued earlier local traditions, suggests that the population did not change. The same burial traditions continued in eastern Bosnia, but here the metal fashions changed and solid bracelets with incised ornament and spiral wire bangles have been found at Glasinac in Benać and Čović's Period IIa-b.[17]

Further north and west in the Save and Drave Valleys, tumuli as at Brgevo Gora were now made to cover cremated and in-urned burials. Tumuli from this period are also found in Dalmatia, the coastal ranges of Croatia and Istria, but cover inhumations accompanied by local

Figs. 46, 47

pottery. In Istria, at sites like Novigrad stone cists encircled by stones were used.

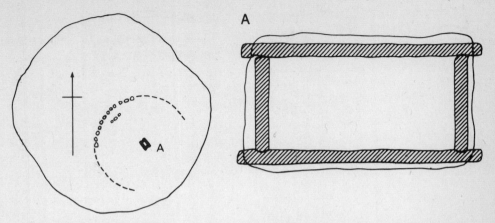

Fig. 46 *Plan of a round barrow with enlargement of the cist which is 1.12 m. long; Monte val Marin (after Messerschmidt)*

Fig. 47 *Section through the stone-lined and covered grave 81 at Pula. c. 1 : 16 (after Messerschmidt)*

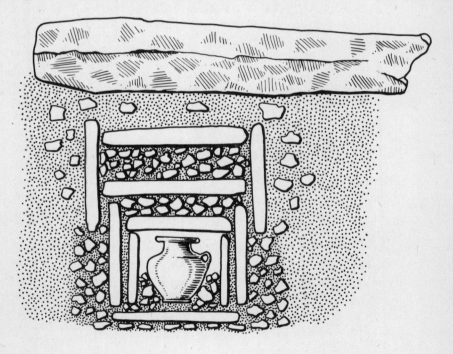

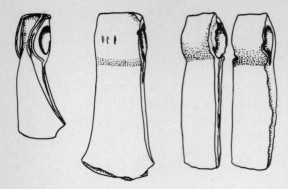

Fig. 48 Bronze shaft-hole axes from a, Debelo Brdo; b, Sobunar; c, Mačkovac (after Sestieri). c. 1 : 4

Fig. 48

In other regions the local peoples seem to have survived relatively unchanged through this period. In Slovenia the long-established Ljubljansko Barje Culture, at sites like Ig yields encrusted pottery of Croatian style as well as dirks, rapiers, razors and shaft-hole axes of Middle Bronze Age types. The latter are also found along the Adriatic coasts and show how popular the Central European metal types had become.

In Bosnia a long-lived settlement, Donja Dolina on a bluff above the south bank of the Save, might well have begun in this period. Much of the pottery of the first occupation was in the Vučedol tradition with tunnel handles and encrusted or incised curvilinear ornament. The stone objects included shaft-hole polygonal battle-axes and flint arrow-heads and a hoard of metal objects of Middle Bronze Age types. In the cave of Hrastovača pottery of the same tradition was also found with bone cheek-pieces for pony harness and shaft-hole axes.[18]

THE LATE BRONZE AGE (*c.* 1200–700 BC)

This period is much richer in remains than any previous one, there being not only settlements and their cemeteries but also specialized military, religious and industrial sites.

It corresponds, in the Aegean coastlands, with the period of swift collapse of the Mycenaean bronze-using civilization (1200–1050) and of the slow rise of the Classical iron-using one (1050–700). Aegean influences became almost non-existent in Jugoslavia after 1150 BC and are not found again until after 800 BC when Greek types begin to be found in Macedonia and Bosnia.

In the rest of Europe, including Jugoslavia, there was also a delay before iron-using became common and, especially in the Eastern Alps, North Italy and the Middle Danube Basin, there were flourishing Late Bronze Age industries which reached new peaks of productivity and inventiveness. Jugoslavia benefited from close contact with both of them, and although the Middle Danubian influence was the strongest for most of the period and reached even to the Adriatic coasts, North Italian/ Alpine influence was always strong in Slovenia.

Fig. 49

Towards the end of the period, in the ninth century, the new and growing influence of Italian cultures (Villanovan, Attestine and Picene) can be noted in Slovenia and Croatia.

In the same century the effects in eastern Jugoslavia of mounted raiders (the Thrako-Cimmerians) from the south Russian steppes become evident.

The most significant internal event of the period was the continued movement of 'Urnfield' peoples from the Middle Danube Basin, and as before, it seems likely that the movements did not stop at the Jugoslav frontiers. When the Dalmatian coasts were reached, for example, they continued by sea and land to eastern Italy, and the 'Japydes' of Apulia, to name one of the best documented groups, probably arrived there during this time. Other groups moved to the south and may be recog- nised during this time at Vergina and at other sites in Greek Macedonia. The probability of these being the 'Illyrian'-speakers known in these regions in the Iron Age is discussed on page 99.

Throughout the whole country in this period new techniques and resources were coming into use. Mining, with shafts and fire-setting (whereby the rock was shattered by lighting fires underneath it) was being practised in the Alps and it is likely that the Jugoslav reserves of copper, gold and silver, particularly in Bosnia and Slovenia, were equally expertly exploited.[19] Smelting and finishing practices now included the use of lead, which lowered the melting point; there was increased use of three-piece moulds, of *cire-perdue* casting and of refined techniques of hammering, rivetting and annealing.

Plate 31

Fig. 38

Whilst the detailed history of the industry remains to be worked out by analysis and typological study, it seems probable that local smiths were already serving local markets with local ores, and that they were using ideas from distant regions. Ornaments, especially brooches, became

Fig. 49   Middle and Late Bronze Age sites

1 Belegiš	28 Krehin Gradac	57 Ripac
2 Beravci	29 Kompolje	58 Ruše
3 Belotić	30 Kulin Vakuf	59 Slatina
4 Bingula Divos	31 Livno	60 Sitno
5 Bijelo Brdo	32 Lukavac	61 Slepšek
6 Bled	33 Makarška	62 Strpči
7 Bizovac	34 Mačkovac	63 Sumetač
8 Bubanj Hum	35 Mokrin	64 Surčin
9 Crvena Stijena	36 Mokronog	65 Sv. Skočijan
10 Čungar	37 Kaštel	66 Sviloš
11 Dalj	38 Nin	67 Šarengrad
12 Debelo Brdo	39 Novigrad	68 Štinjan
13 Dobova	40 Omoljica	69 Tenja
14 Dobračs	41 Osor	70 Tešanj
15 Donja Dolina	42 Otok Privlaka	71 Tetovo
16 Dubovac	43 Paraćin	72 Tiščovac
17 Dubravica	44 Pečina	73 Temeš Kubin
18 Dupljaja	45 Peringrad	74 Unesić
19 Glasinac; Drenovo Do,	46 Pocravlje i Brod	75 Vattina
Gucevo, Kovacev Do,	47 Podzemelj	76 Virak
Osovo, Podilijak,	48 Porec	77 Vinča
Taline, Vrlazije	49 Pričac	78 Vintian
20 Gračanica	50 Pančevo	79 Vermo
21 Hrustovača Pećina	51 Prilep	80 Velike Humska Cuka
22 Ig	52 Privlaka (Otok)	81 Vukovar
23 Ilandža	53 Probrizje	82 Zadar
24 Jajce	54 Prozor	83 Zencovi
25 Kličevac	55 Ptuj	84 Žlatište
26 Korbovo	56 Požarevac	85 Žuto Brdo
27 Kumanovo		

Fig. 51

increasingly popular and provide excellent indicators of both date and cultural connections, for there were from the beginning of the period recognizable Middle Danubian and Central European, and before the end, Italian and Greek fashions.

Among the weapons, tongue-grip swords were now common and five groups, including a 'Slavonian' type, have been distinguished;[20] but there were still solid-hilted swords of Hungarian type. The forms of socketed spears with incised ornament and of shaft-hole battle-axes with slightly drooping blades originated in the Danube Basin but palstaves

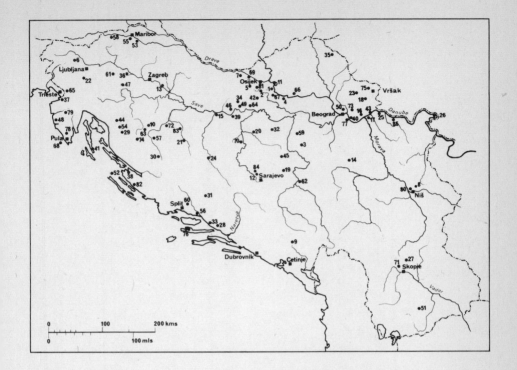

Fig. 50

of Central European type were also used. Tanged sickles and socketed axes, usually with cast loops and ornament, are now common, the wide varieties of shape and ornament suggesting that there were a number of regional traditions. Another new tool was the single-edged knife, very often with a tanged handle.

The effect of the new forms upon everyday life must have been consider- able for tools like sickles, knives and axes were being produced in large numbers.

The dating of these events is made somewhat easier by a great variety of metal types and the copying of Italian as well as Central European and Middle Danubian fashions. As a result, a division valid for Jugo- slavia as a whole can be made at about 1000 BC. *Late Bronze Age I* (1200–1000) was contemporary with the Central European Hallstatt A, the Hungarian Bronze Age IV–V, and the Greek Mycenaean IIIc/ Proto-Geometric periods. *Late Bronze Age II* (1000–750 BC) was contemporary with the Central European Hallstatt B, the Hungarian

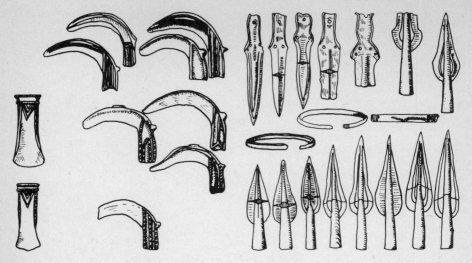

Fig. 50 A selection of bronze weapons, ornaments and tools from the 128 objects found in the Late Bronze Age hoard at Tenja (after Holske). c. 1 : 5

Bronze Age VI – Thrako-Cimmerian, the Greek Geometric and the Italian Villanovan I-II periods.[21]

It would be unwise to adopt any of these neighbouring nomenclatures in Jugoslavia since the concordances are not exact; local subdivisions in most regions of Jugoslavia have been successfully made and will be used here.

Pannonian Culture On the southern margins of the Danube Plain, as in neighbouring Hungary, there is at this time no evidence of any change of population and the Pannonian Culture, as the cremating, urn-using groups of Dubovac, Vrsac, Žuto Brdo and Vattina may now be called, continued; there was, however, a considerable mixing of 'urnfield' and 'tumulus' rites in cemeteries like Ilandza and Vukovar. Defensible sites seem to have come more into favour and at settlements like Dalja and Dubravica, the small rectangular houses were built on bluffs above rivers or on hill-tops.[22] From the same region come many hoards of bronze objects; most contain broken or partially-melted fragments and must have belonged to smiths or founders. They are concentrated near the confluences of the Rivers Danube, Save, Drave and Morava and the majority come from the end of the period (the Hallstatt A2 phase of the Central European chronology).[23] Of special significance are the large

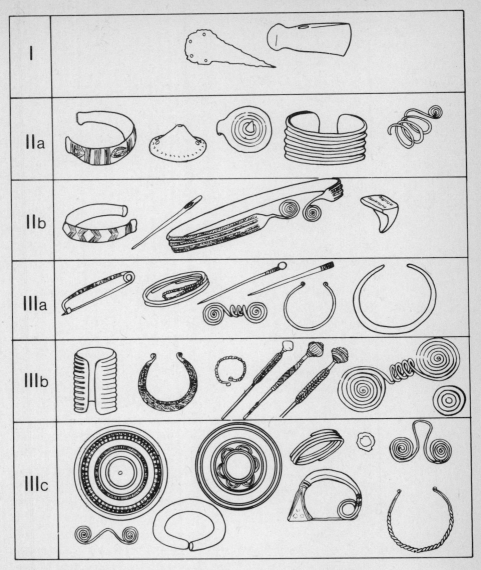

Fig. 51   The Benac and Čović typology of pre 750 BC bronzes from the Glasinac cemeteries

numbers of tanged sickles and socketed axes for they are the first indication of metal being common enough for everyday tools. Many of the fashions and ideas, even in Serbia, have spread from the eastern Alps and include winged axes and palstaves, single-edged knives with curved backs, arm-rings, spears and safety-pin brooches. Hoards like Otok Privlaka, Bingula Divos, Boscovac and Sviloš also contain Middle Danubian mushroom-headed pins, socketed axes and brooches of 'Posamentarie' type, whilst from Pozarevac comes the earliest of a series of fine cauldrons made of riveted bronze sheets. There are no signs of any Italian or Greek influence.

Migrations to the South It seems very likely that the movement of peoples from the Middle Danube Basin into Greek Macedonia and Epirus continued. The Morava Valley, the natural route to the south, has little direct evidence of this, although some pottery of Vattina type has been found, and hoards of bronzes at Jajčić and Gučevo (Serbia), and Kumanovo and Prilep (Macedonia) contain northern forms. [24] It is only south of the Balkan Mountains in the Vadar Basin that good evidence is found in settlements like Vadaroftsa, cemeteries like Vergina, and hoards like Gribiani. A Group (C) of tumuli at Vergina may well belong to this period for there were no iron objects, and the fluted dark-faced pottery was of Middle Danubian type. At Vadaroftsa similar pottery was found with iron slag in the burnt debris of a Mycenaean (IIIc) settlement.[25] There is reason to suppose that these groups of invaders played some part in dislodging the Greek-speaking Dorians, and that they were among the ancestors of the historic Macedonians and Epirotes.

In the mountains of Slovenia, Croatia, Bosnia and western Serbia the inhabitants, although subjected to invasion from the Danube Plains, seem to have preserved most of their older traditions. In western Serbia, for example, the earlier Serbian Tumulus Culture between the Morava and Drina Valleys continued, and mounds of up to 20 metres in diameter covering stone circles around inhumations, or more rarely cremations, are found. In eastern Bosnia, where the material and cemeteries have been studied by Čovič and Benać, the Glasinac Valley was still the main burial place for many communities.[26] Most of the older rites prevailed and burial continued, as it did until Roman times, to take the form of inhumation surrounded by stones under a tumulus. The grave goods of

Plate 32

Fig. 54

this period (Glasinac IIIb) include 'cuff' bracelets, incised neckrings, elaborate pins and socketed axes (as at Drenovi Do and Sumetic) of Middle Danube type. Contemporary graves have also been found in Montenegro at Vodhine in the Upper Drina Valley.

Fig. 51

More certainly immigrant groups can be traced to the west in Bosnia. At Donja Dolina, the settlement on the bluff overlooking the Save, pottery which included biconic urns and small high-handled bowls was now used, as well as tanged sickles, decorated spears and tanged swords matched in east Croatia. At the hill-top of Zencovi (Prijedor) one urnfield settlement was now succeeded by another with pottery ornamented by channelling in Dubova-Žuto Brdo Culture style.[27] A few urnfields like Gracanica in Bosnia even show the full Middle Danubian lowland burial rites. Middle Danubian connections are also shown by the metal objects from Peringrad and Debelo Brdo.

Similar objects are found in hoards in Hercegovina and western Croatia; for example at Tešanj and Todsovice (Mostar), Krehin Gradac, Kulen Vakuf, Tiscovac and Pecina. Here, in the valleys behind the coastal mountains there is evidence of increased settlement, and a number of burials under tumuli, shrines and hill-top settlements are known. At Unešić, for example, a tumulus covered an inhumation furnished with a disc-footed safety-pin.[28] A different rite is illustrated by the cemetery and shrine in the cave of Miroslavlijic; this like that of Skočijan clearly shows that there was some continuity in this region from the later Bronze Age to Roman times.[29]

Dalmatia seems more affected by coastal movements of ideas and peoples than by movements from the interior. In the north, a number of settlements and cemeteries in Istria have yielded pottery with applied cordons and elaborately-crested handles like some found further south in Dalmatia and in the Apennine Bronze Age of Italy.[30]

Fig. 52

Castilieri Culture The fortification of settlements with drystone walls, 'castilieri', as at Monte Vitian was now becoming necessary and was to remain so for centuries (p. 95). A hoard of medial-winged axes from Monte Maesta, and scattered socketed axes and tanged sickles elsewhere show connections with inland Slovenia and Croatia, as do the earliest objects (a tongue-grip sword, decorated spears, shaft-hole and socketed axes) from the cave of Sv. Skočijan. This cave was a shrine at which some twelve hundred offerings were made through the centuries.[31]

Farther south, in Dalmatia, the bronze finds of this period also resemble those of the east Alpine and Middle Danube regions. Socketed and shaft-hole axes, tongue-grip swords and spears with sinuous-edged blades are found on at least twenty-six sites on the coasts and islands. In central Dalmatia settlements like Sali and Privlaka, and cemeteries like Vrsi can be dated to this period. It has been suggested that it was by this coastal route that some objects, especially tongue-grip swords, socketed axes and sinuous-edged spear-heads, reached Greece in the twelfth and eleventh centuries.[32]

Across the Adriatic in northeastern Italy some of the urnfields and metal hoards of the Proto and Early Villanovan period may well be related.[33]

This period, in which there was much disturbance among the peoples of Central Europe, witnessed the destruction of some of the Middle Danubian Bronze Age cultures and the rise of vigorous Greek and Italian iron-using civilizations. These events were reflected in Jugoslavia.

In the Danube Basin, in northern Serbia and eastern Croatia, no great change took place before the eighth century BC. A large number of hoards of bronze objects show that the local industry was at its highest point of development between 1000 and 850 BC (the Hallstatt B1 and especially B2 phases of the Central European chronology).[34] The hoards were very large and at Beravci, for example, among several hundred objects there were seventeen varieties of socketed axes and nine of tanged sickles. Single-edged knives, swords and ornaments were also common. These were presumably being used by the Urnfield cultures although bronze objects are not normally found in the cemeteries.

Fig. 50

Thrako-Cimmerian Raiders The evidence from 850 to 750 BC (the Hallstatt B3 phase of Central Europe) shows the arrival of mounted and probably cart-driving peoples from southern Russia in this region. These, called in Childe's rather unfortunate phrase 'Thrako-Cimmerians', were iron-users and are discussed in the next chapter (p. 118). Since the cemeteries and large metal hoards are no longer found it is likely that, as elsewhere, the Thrako-Cimmerians were raiders and destroyers.

Connections with Greek Macedonia and the Lower Danube Basin were, however, maintained through this time. The incursions of the raiders may even have resulted in increased mobility, but there is no evidence of large-scale population movements. At Vergina, for example, metal forms common in Serbia and Bosnia throughout this period, including 'spectacle' brooches, continue to be found. Similar and contemporary finds come from the Basarabi Culture (phases I and II) of Romania and show that there too, links with Jugoslavia were maintained.[35]

Another development of the ninth and eighth centuries was that ideas and objects began to spread from the south and west after a gap of several centuries. In Jugoslav Macedonia, Bosnia and Serbia, Greek fashions in ornament were probably coming into use, whilst Italian ones were beginning to appear in Dalmatia and as far east as Dalja and Donja Dolina in the Save Valley.

Urnfield invasions from the north In northern Jugoslavia the most significant event of this period was the arrival of groups from Central Europe, for one route taken by the restless Alpine 'Urnfielders' brought them into the Upper Save and Drave Basins. As in earlier and later times in Jugoslavia, this resulted not in the complete replacement of one people by another, but in an intermingling and the rise of new groupings.

Fig. 52   Urns from the Pula cemetery. c. 1 : 6 (after Messerschmidt)

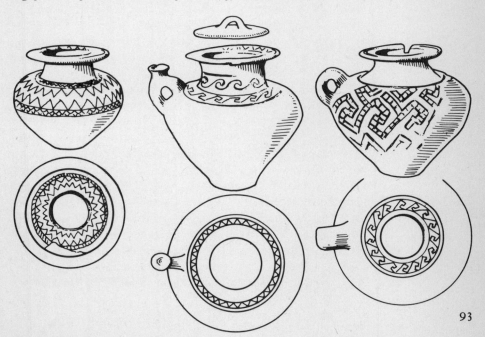

Fig. 53

Near the Austrian frontier the Prištava cemetery at Bled gives a good idea of the varieties of burial ritual practised at this time, for six types of cremation burial were found with three cremating areas (pyres) and three 'ritual' areas, with animal but no human bones.[36] Farther south at Dobova another cremation cemetery with stone-lined flat graves had cylindrical-necked two-handled pots which can be paralleled in Austria. Cemeteries at Ptuj, Probrezje, Ruše and Ljubljana had similar pottery. The metal objects, including conical and globe-headed pins, 'spectacle' and 'harp' brooches, were all of Alpine type.[37]

Hoards of metal objects are rare in north Jugoslavia and show mostly Alpine influence but the hoard from Bled, with tanged sickles, middle- and end-winged axes suggests that in Slovenia metal was common enough for everyday tools. Fine ornamented spear-heads of this period have been dredged from the river at Ljubljana whilst 'spectacle' brooches came from Dobova. In central Croatia, fortified hill-top settlements had now become necessary. They and the tumuli are dated by imported metal objects from farther north or west. The finds in the Lika Valley at Kompolje and at Prozor suggest that connections with Italy through the passes in the coastal ranges were already in existence. Since there seems to be no break for centuries in the continuity of sites like Prozor, it may well be that the Japodes, the tribe found here in the Early Iron Age (p. 111), were already present and that they controlled part of the sea coast.[38] If so, these invaders were presumably Illyrian-speaking (p. 99).

The migration from the East Alpine region does not seem to have reached as far down the Save and Drave Valleys as the Later Celtic-speaking invaders, nor to have greatly affected the mountainous regions of Bosnia and Hercegovina. At Zagreb (Horvati), for example, a cremation cemetery of stone-lined flat graves contained biconic and sharply-carinated pottery with channelled ornament which had its best parallels at Dalja and Donja Dolina.[39]. Even as far north as Mokronog, Slavonian-type pottery was made and tumulus burial was practised into the full Iron Age (p. 109).

Attestine Culture On the coastlands and islands of the Adriatic Sea other groups can be recognized. At the head of the Adriatic in the Venetian Plain the Attestine Culture, later to be attributed to the Veneti, appears before the end of the period. Its ceramic work has connections in Slovenia at Ljubljana and Podzemelj, whilst its metalwork is of

North Italian type. Like so many other historically-known tribes, the Veneti may have been formed at this time of a mixture of peoples.

The Istrian peninsula seems to have retained older traditions, for the settlements concentrated near the coasts and the tumuli covering inhumations continue to have pottery with applied cordons and crested handles; Paravija kod Babarije may be considered typical of the period. The cave shrine of Sv. Skočijan continued to be venerated, the offerings including fine Italian brooches and palstaves. Most of the settlements are now fortified and some, like the double-walled settlement of Monte Castellier on the island of Brijuni, show great constructional skill.[40]

From further south a group of new settlements at Nin, Zadar and Radovin seem to begin in this period and to continue into full historic times. Their cemeteries contained cordoned pottery and the bronze objects, some of inland type, are best paralleled in Slovenia.[41] It may well be that the Liburni, who are known to have been here *c.* 750 BC, were already present.

Migration beyond the sea This is the most likely period for the arrival in Italy of the groups with Balkan affinities: Picenes, Daunians, Peucetians and Massapians, who were settled along the whole eastern coast in about

Fig. 53 Plan of part of the cemetery at Bled showing the variety of burial rites (after Gabrovic)

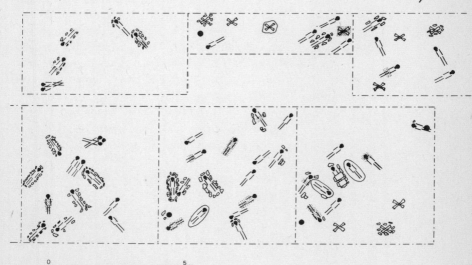

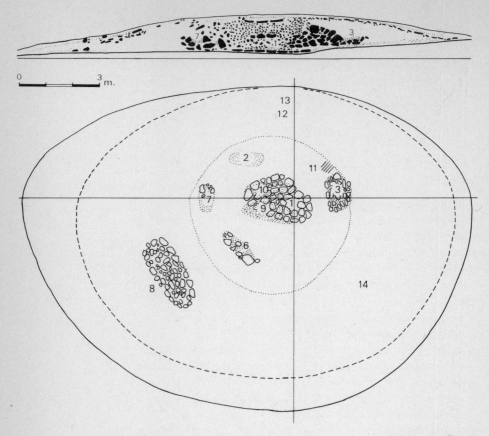

Fig. 54   Plan and section of a barrow, Podilijak A, from the Glasinac cemeteries (after Čović)

750 BC. The distinctive Picene Culture may be recognised as early as the ninth century when a number of Central European and Balkan forms are found there. Farther south at Coppa Nevigata and Grotta Macaccora (level III) the pottery has many parallels with Donja Dolina, Debelo Brdo, Dalja and Ripac. In Apulia the tribal name, Japydes, which was also used by the Romans for the Japodes of Croatia, is encountered and metal objects, especially shaft-hole axes of Balkan type, are found.

The possibility of a trade route along the Dalmatian coast has already been discussed (p. 77); it might at this time be linked with the Illyrian-

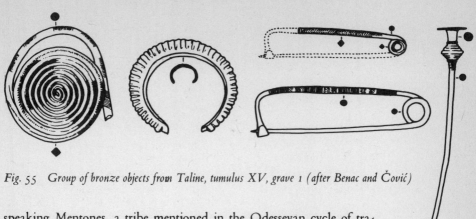

Fig. 55   Group of bronze objects from Taline, tumulus XV, grave 1 (after Benac and Čović)

speaking Mentones, a tribe mentioned in the Odesseyan cycle of traditions. Other currents of trade brought Italian objects to Dalmatia and
Slovenia in the ninth and eighth centuries[42] and these are found along
the routes through the coastal mountains which were to be used so much
in future centuries. Greek fashions also began to appear in the south;
two early serpentine brooches from Nin suggest the Greek colonies in
Sicily and some of the arc brooches with large catch-plates from
Hercegovina and Bosnia copy Greek mainland ones of the eighth
century. In Bosnia and Hercegovina existing populations were not
disturbed by migrations, for there is continuity at a whole series of sites.[43]
At Donja Dolina and Zencovi, for example, the settlements continued,
although at Donja Dolina the metalwork included Italian-style lunate
razors and urn-burial was practised, while at Zencovi there was an influx
of Donja Dolina-type pottery. Hill-top settlements, usually with fortifications, and riverside dwellings supported on piles became more
common and are found, as at Ripac, not only in central but also, as at
Zlatiska and Čungar (Cazin), in southern Bosnia.

The main cemeteries west of the Bosna Valley were still concentrated
in the Glasinac area and continued to use the old burial rites through the
whole period. The metal objects in the graves included Italian and Greek
fashions in brooches and those at Strbči, Osovo and Gučevo may be
instanced as typical finds. The hoards of bronze objects as at Drenovi Do
and Grapska also contained Italian types.

Figs. 54, 55

97

CHAPTER V

The Pre-Roman Iron Age

During the last seven centuries before the completion of the Roman Conquest which marks the limit of our survey, Jugoslavia was a close neighbour of civilized, literate, urban peoples in both Italy and Greece. During this time, trading relationships grew steadily stronger and literary evidence is added to the archaeological remains. As a result a more detailed history can be compiled than for any previous period and from it three points of considerable significance emerge.

The western regions, especially the Dalmatian coast, were richer, more populous and more important than ever before. Through the mountain passes Italian goods, recognizably from Venetia, Tuscany, Marche and Apulia, and Greek goods from the Greek mainland and colonies in southern Italy and Sicily, reached the interior. For these, slaves, amber, minerals and other products of East and Central Europe were exchanged. This trade pattern was very different from that of the previous centuries in which even the Adriatic coasts followed the fashions of the Middle Danubian and East Alpine regions (p. 84). It was as complete a change as that found in West Africa after the opening of the sea routes in the sixteenth century AD and perhaps had similarly dramatic effects.[1]

Secondly, over much of the region there is no evidence of extensive movements of peoples. The settlements and cemeteries remain in use for many generations and show a stable, prosperous and numerous population. Only in the Middle Danube Basin was there a considerable invasion. This stability means that a number of tribal groups reported on by Greeks and Romans can be recognized several centuries before they became truly historic.

Fig. 57

Thirdly, the great increase in trade and the quick adoption of foreign fashions throw much light on the regional groupings, overseas connections and chronology of the prehistoric tribes. They show that while the land routes northwards from Greece were long blocked to trade, although some objects and ideas filtered through, the land routes eastwards from north Italy were much used. Advantage was also taken of the sea routes throughout the whole period and two of particular importance can be distinguished: west-east across the Adriatic Sea from

Marche to central Dalmatia and south-north up the Adriatic from the Aegean to the Po Valley. Beyond Jugoslavia to the north, the land routes through Central Europe were open.

ILLYRIANS, ILLYRIA AND ILLYRICUM

A number of the tribes of this period have been accepted, because of the unbroken cultural traditions extending into historic times, as 'Illyrians'. This imprecise and often confusing term should be used to mean Illyrian-speakers, for Illyrian languages are well known to have been one of the main sub-divisions of the Indo-European language family within the Roman Empire.[2] From the seventh century BC groups with elements of this language were known in eastern Italy, northern Greece and Albania, Jugoslavia and uncertain regions beyond. The name Illyria, however, was at first reserved both by Greeks and Romans for the south Jugoslav-Albania region near the Greek frontier and the Adriatic Sea. It was only in 35 BC at the creation of the much-enlarged Roman province of 'Illyricum' that the term was applied to most of Jugoslavia, and from the first it included Celtic-speaking peoples.

THE COMING OF IRON TO JUGOSLAVIA

Iron was coming into common usage along the northern coasts of the Aegean and Black Sea by about 1000 BC and into much of Italy between 900–800 BC. It was in common use in Jugoslavia by *c.* 700 BC, The knowledge of it having spread during the previous three centuries.[3] *Fig. 56*
The earliest iron objects, as might be expected, were few, small and widely scattered, and, like so many of the contemporary bronze objects, suggest that the knowledge of iron-using came to much of Jugoslavia via the Dalmatian coast and Venetian plain at the head of the Adriatic. The evidence suggests that it came almost by chance as part of the cultural equipment of traders, much as it came to the Pacific islands in the seventeenth century AD. The slowness of the acceptance of iron by local peoples seems due partly to a lack of trading relationships before the eighth century BC and partly to the existence of good supplies of bronze in much of Jugoslavia. As has been seen, bronze had already been used for farm tools for several centuries so that in no sense did iron at once cause a revolution in the way of life of the people; it only slowly replaced bronze even for tools and weapons.

Jugoslavia

Fig. 56 Sites of the Iron Age in Jugoslavia

1 Atenica	36 Korčula	72 Ribniačka
2 Baška	37 Kostolac	73 Rijeka
3 Barajevo	38 Kostrevnica	74 Ribić
4 Beograd	39 Kotor	75 Ripač
5 Beravci	40 Kompolje	76 Rospi Čuprija
6 Bitolj	41 Križna Gora	77 Rudnik
7 Bihać	42 Libna	78 Rudovci
8 Bled	43 Ljubljana	79 Rtanj
9 Brač	44 Magdalenska Gora	80 Ruše
10 Brestovik	45 Mahrevice	81 Sanski Most
11 Brezje	46 Maribor	82 Šarengrad
12 Budva	47 Medak	83 Slankamen
13 Čurug	48 Mazin	84 Šibenik
14 Cres	49 Malino	85 Sisak
15 Dalj	50 Metiković	86 Solin
16 Debelo Brdo	51 Mitrovice	87 Sotin
17 Demir Kapija	52 Mramorac	88 Stari Grad (Hvar)
18 Djevdjalja	53 Mokronog	89 Stična; Sv. Vid
19 Donja Dolina	54 Momišići; Medum	90 Stobi
20 Dubovac	55 Monte Maesta	91 Strbči
21 Drešinja Vas	56 Nin	92 Sv. Skočijan (S. Canziano)
22 Duvno kod Gaja	57 Novi Banovci	93 Sv. Lucija (S. Lucia)
23 Glasinac; Citluci,	58 Novi Pazar	94 Trebenište
Ilijak, Osovo,	59 Novo Mesto	95 Ulaka
Rusanovice, Zagradje	60 Osijek	96 Vrsi
24 Gorica	61 Osanić	97 Vače
25 Gornja Stražava	62 Osor	98 Vičja Luka
26 Grude	63 Paraćin	99 Vinča
27 Hrustovača Pećina	64 Pičugi	100 Vinica
28 Hvar	65 Pod kod Bogojno	101 Vizace; Nesazio
29 Idrija pri Bači	66 Podgradje (Asseria)	102 Vital
30 Ig	67 Podzemelj	103 Viš
31 Jajce	68 Probrižje	104 Vermo
32 Jeserine	69 Prozor	105 Zadar
33 Jošanička Banja	70 Pula	106 Zaton
34 Kladova	71 Radolište	108 Židovar
35 Knin		

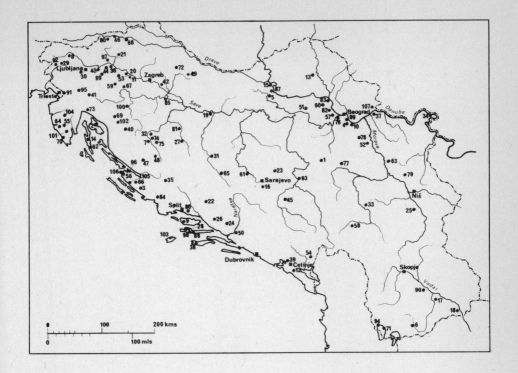

The Middle Danube Basin may have acquired its knowledge of iron in a less peaceful way. Some of the 'Thrako-Cimmerian' horse-riding peoples who were found in Hungary and Romania in the ninth-eighth centuries (p. 92) knew iron, and although they did not penetrate far into Jugoslavia, their raids may have introduced the new metal.[4] Even so the forms taken by some of the earliest iron objects in the Save Valley, like those at Sisak, Šarengrad and Ruše, resemble Italian ones of the same centuries.

The choice by archaeologists of the point at which iron became common as the moment of transition from one 'Age' to another can be seen to be purely of chronological convenience. The conventional divisions of the Jugoslav Iron Age have generally followed those of Central Europe: the earlier 'Hallstatt' Iron Age, sub-divided into 'C' (c. 750–600) and 'D' (600–450); and the later 'La Tène' into 'I' (c. 450–300), 'II' (300–100) and 'III' (100–11 BC). Over much of Jugoslavia such a division is

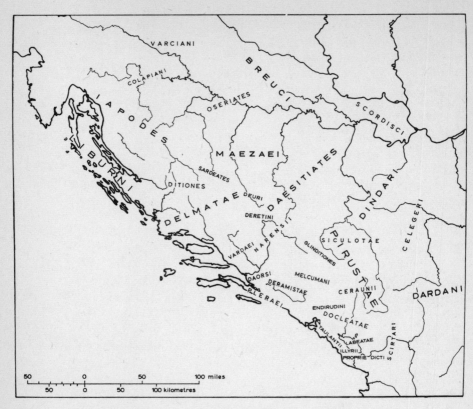

Fig. 57   *The native peoples of Jugoslavia at the time of the Roman conquest (after Wilkes)*

meaningful only if applied in a different sense and with dates that differ from those of Central Europe, and the terms should be modified. The coincidence, in the fourth century BC, of two of the three main events of the period, the Greek colonisation of Dalmatia and the Celtic invasion of the Middle Danube Basin, means that a division at *c.* 350 BC is widely valid both north and south of the central mountain ranges. North of it the 'Hallstatt' and 'La Tène' nomenclature of Central Europe is still useful, although the commencement of the La Tène period varies from about 450 BC in Slovenia to 300 BC in Serbia. South of the mountains, in Dalmatia and Montenegro, and in southern Serbia and Macedonia a division can also be made about 350–330 BC, at the time of increased Greek colonial activity.

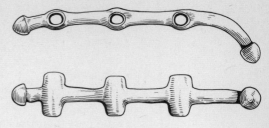

Fig. 58 Bronze cheek-piece from a horse bridle, Dalj. Length 16 cms (after Gallus and Horvath)

On either side of the mountains, the two periods might equally well be called Iron Age I and II, for it is possible to assign absolute dates to their sub-divisions through the finding of Greek and Italian imports. Even in the central mountains, the least-affected region, this division can be used.

EARLY IRON AGE I (c. 700–350 BC)

Throughout Jugoslavia, this period is really defined by its metal typology, for most of its other cultural manifestations are continuations from the Late Bronze Age. Of the objects found, those made of bronze were often ornaments of pride and high fashion and show the greatest regional variations. Among the brooches, for example, there were 'loop-bow', 'large catch-plate', 'spectacle', and 'crossbow' classes, which were popular in different regions of Jugoslavia. Many varieties of ordinary pins were also used and 'globe-', 'cone-' and 'ladder-headed' as well as 'double-shanked' forms are especially interesting.[5] The use of iron was restricted to simple objects, mainly weapons and tools of which lug-adzes, sabres and socketed axes were the most significant.

Fig. 58

Fig. 60

Fig. 61

Fig. 59

Among the rest of the evidence the ceramic forms common in the Late Bronze Age continued, but Italian and Greek wheel-made forms became increasingly popular. The burial customs developed local combinations of earlier cremation and inhumation rituals with a wide variety of accompanying rites, and burials were often covered by tumuli.[6] A few very rich graves suggest a developing class structure and by the end of the period there were literary references to 'kings' controlling considerable areas. Hill-top fortifications of great elaboration and riverside settlements on piles were now common.

Plates 36, 38

Plates 33–35

Attestine Culture Each of the main regions will be discussed in turn. The Adriatic Coastlands have now become of major importance and must be considered first. On the northern shores of the Adriatic Sea, all through the period, the distinctive Attestine Culture dominated the

Venetian Plain and much of Istria and the Julian Alps in western
Slovenia. There is little doubt that this represents the Veneti, apparently
an Italic-speaking tribe, whom contemporary literature reported as
trading widely into Central and Eastern Europe. One of their trade routes
led through Slovenia, and in the foothills of the Julian Alps, especially
in the Soča Valley, cemeteries and hill-forts of this period are known.[7]
At one of them, Sv. Lucija, a very large cemetery in which some 7000
graves have already been excavated,[8] most of the graves were cremations
in pits, sometimes stone-lined. The ashes were accompanied by urns and
jewellery, especially bronze safety-pins and necklaces of amber and glass
beads. Many of the objects were of well-known eighth- to fifth-century

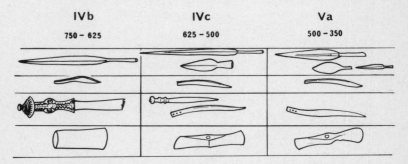

IVb	IVc	Va
750 – 625	625 – 500	500 – 350

*Figs. 59, 60 Iron weapons and bronze safety-pins from the Glasinac cemeteries,
arranged chronologically (after Benac and Čović)*

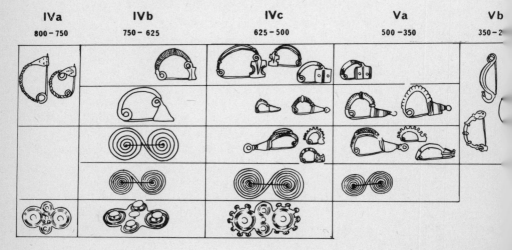

IVa	IVb	IVc	Va	Vb
800 – 750	750 – 625	625 – 500	500 – 350	350 – 2

BC Italian types, coming mostly from the Po Valley but with some from central and southern Italy. Central European types were also common, but Greek objects were few and late (fifth century BC).

In the coastal regions from Trieste to Rijeka other contemporary cemeteries and stone-walled settlements (*castillieri*) are known and the pottery links them with Slovenia and even with Bosnia. The Bronze Age shrine at Sv. Skočijan (p. 91) still continued to attract votive offerings.

In the Istrian peninsula there is evidence of a considerable population at this time, for many of the three hundred and fifty fortified settlements and refuges – some with associated cemeteries of tumuli or flat graves –

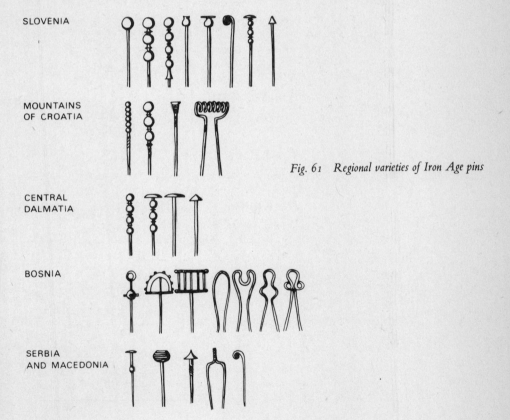

Fig. 61   *Regional varieties of Iron Age pins*

which have been located were in use.[9] Of the objects found, a division can be made between a northwest and a southeast group, the former linking with Slovenia and Venetia and the latter with the islands of Cres and Krk, and with central Dalmatia. A good example of these settlements has been excavated at Pičugi where a triple-ramparted contour-fort had a cemetery of five hundred cremation graves of this period between the first and second walls. Other excavated examples are Monte Ursino (Pula) where one of the two ramparts of squared stone still stands 5 metres high and where there was a cemetery near by, and Nezakcij (the classical Nezactium) where, with much other evidence, there were sophisticated sculptures in stone. These included human torsos, a horseman, and squared blocks with incised boss, spiral and swastika designs dating to the sixth-fifth centuries BC.[10] As in the Soča Valley the typology of the metal objects shows close links with the Este region in the Po Valley between 700 and 500 BC, but relatively few Greek or southern Italian imports were in evidence even where there was a Greek trading post at Spina near the mouth of the River Po.[11]

Southeast of Istria, in central and southern Dalmatia, the islands and the coastal plain also now supported a larger population. Krk and Cres in the north have fine stone-walled settlements and large cemeteries. Osor on Cres is a good example, for the cemetery seems to have been in use from the eighth to the first century BC and to have had closer connections with eastern central Italy (the classical Picenum) and the Zadar region of Dalmatia than with Istria. On the mainland of central Dalmatia in the rich plains around Zadar more than sixty-seven sites of this period are known, the most important being Nin, where some seventy-two inhumation graves, many lined and covered with stones, can be dated to the eighth-fourth centuries.[12] At Nin, Zaton and Orsi there were very strong connections with the Ancona-Rimini region of Italy. This showed especially in the bronze brooches, pendants, and razors, and in the style of the amber necklaces. There are few Greek objects from these sites and none earlier than the sixth century BC. The linguistic, literary and archaeological evidence for trans-Adriatic links are so close that movement across the Adriatic can be accepted.

The Liburni There is also no doubt that the Liburni are represented by the Jugoslav evidence. They were powerful as visitors and even conquerors as far south as Corfu in the seventh century and their trade connections reached far inland. They were still living in central Dalmatia under the Empire.[13]

South of Šibenik other tribes are known from the later Iron Age and it is probable that the Delmatae, Ardiei and Pleraei were already present. From the islands of Viš, Korčula and especially Mlec come finds of this period, well dated after 600 BC by Greek imports. Trading into the interior of Bosnia and Hercegovina was already considerable, although not apparently dominated by any one coastal tribe.

The Greeks in Dalmatia before 400 BC   Greek colonies and even influence in central and northern Dalmatia seems non-existent before 600 BC and slight until after 400 BC; the reasons for this have been much debated. Corfu, controlled by Euboeans, was prosperous in the late eighth and extremely powerful in the sixth century, but Epidamnus, in Albania (Durazzo), was, before the fourth century BC, the most northerly well-established Greek colony. This town was only founded in 626 BC. In Dalmatia there was only the semi-piratical venture of a group of Cnidians and Rhodians who are reported to have settled on Korčula in 580–570 BC.[14] No coins were certainly struck and the settlement suspected at Vučja Luka has not yet been found so that its continued existence after that decade is suspect.

The various explanations for the lack of Greek settlement on the Dalmatian coast – that it was not polis (city) country, that its rainfall was too heavy or its storms too unpredictable – are unconvincing in view of its later history. Perhaps the reports of piracy, a possible synonym for native hostility, and a strong cross-Adriatic trading partnership for which there is archaeological evidence were the real causes of the lack of settlement.

The focal point of southern Dalmatian trade was at the mouth of the River Naretva; even triremes could row some ten miles inland, and with its tributaries it was the best route into Bosnia, Hercegovina and northern Montenegro. There is every reason to suppose that this was the region with which the Greeks first traded. It is probably this route that Herodotus meant when he wrote of objects from beyond the Scyths (probably of the Middle Danube Basin) reaching the Adriatic coasts and being carried thence to Dordona in northeastern Greece. The earliest Greek objects on the coast are of the sixth-fifth centuries and stretch from Nin, where an Attic Red-Figure krater is dated to *c.* 480 BC, to Viš, Brač and

Korčula where were found Attic and Corinthian vases and helmets dated to *c.* 400 BC. Vučja Luka on Viš has at present the best claim to have been a settlement of this period.

Italians in Dalmatia before 400 BC Although no colonies from Italy have been found in Dalmatia, the linguistic and cultural ties across the Adriatic were very strong between 700 and 400 BC. A scatter of Italian objects are found along the whole coast but it is in central Dalmatia (Kotori) that the connections were strongest.[15] They linked the region between Ancona and Rimini in Italy, the territory of the Picenes, with that of the Liburni. Besides similar tastes in metal objects both Picenes and Liburni liked amber and these mark the trade routes through Croatia and beyond. Sea battles, as carved on Picene tombstones, and the reputation of the Dalmatian pirates may account for the absence of Greek influence. Farther south, Italian objects are found as far inland as northern and eastern Bosnia. These were presumably traded through the Naretva and Bosna Valleys used also by Greek merchants. Bosnian objects in Apulia and Marche, especially double-shanked pins, must have accompanied the return cargoes. With the increase of Greek trade after 500 BC this southern route was less used by Italians. In northern Dalmatia trans-Adriatic connections were also strong in the islands of Cres and Krk and on the mainland in southeastern Istria.

The Interior In inland Jugoslavia, behind the coastal mountains, there is also evidence of more numerous populations than ever before. They lived in stable communities, and Greek and Italian influence increased as the attraction of the civilizations of the Greeks and Etruscans grew stronger. Since a series of cultural groupings, to some of which tribal names may legitimately be attached, are known, each inland region may be discussed in turn.

In the north in Slovenia the pattern of settlement emerges from Stare's study of more than fifty sites.[16] In the Drave Basin the Late Bronze Age communities (p. 94) continued but new and more flourishing developments were now to be found in the Save Basin, especially that part of it stretching from Ljubljana eastwards to the Croatian border. Iron-using became common in these valleys in the late eighth century, and cemeteries of cremation graves, like those at Prištava (Bled), Ljubljana, Križna Gora and Ruše, have high-necked urns, and Italian metal types of the eighth-seventh centuries as well as new local forms like the loop-bow

Fig. 62

Fig. 62   Pottery from Stični. c. 1 : 3 (after Frey)

brooches. East of Ljubljana the new groups are held by Starè to show continuity with the local Bronze Age, the pottery with its hatched triangles and white encrustation suggesting Slavonian wares (p. 62). Fortified hill-tops and associated cemeteries, some with and some without tumuli but both containing inhumations and cremations alike, are common. At Magdalenska Gora for example, on the hill-sides below an earth-ramparted hill-fort, were several cemeteries of flat graves and tumuli.[17] Each tumulus was in fact a small cemetery, since from the ten excavated came three hundred and thirty-five burials. Some of the graves contained many more objects than others. In a grave in Tumulus VII (sixth century), for example, a woman and child wore amber necklaces and bronze breast ornaments, safety-pins on each shoulder and arm and leg bangles, whilst the occupant of Tumulus V grave 29 was a man equipped with swords and spears, a shield with a circular boss and a knife, all of iron, a bronze torc and an amber necklace; beside him were a bronze bucket and cauldron and an iron spit. Similar cemeteries and settlements have been found at Brezje (Radovlja) and Sv. Vid (Stični). At the latter site a recent excavation showed evidence of complex rituals, for over one hundred separate features including the building of a stone perimeter wall accompanied the burials under a great tumulus. Here locally-made dot-decorated pottery, body armour and ornaments were

Fig. 63

Fig. 63   Bronze cauldron from Magdalenska Gora, tumulus V (after Starè). c. 1 : 5

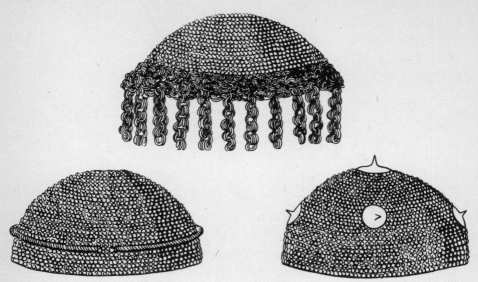

Fig. 64   Leather helmets with metal studs and mail; Krompolje graves 43, 63, 67. c. 3 : 16 (after Dreschler-Bižr

Fig. 64

Fig. 65

Plates 44, 45

Plates 46, 49

accompanied by imported Greek colonial pottery and Etruscan bronzes. The preservation of organic matter meant that bronze-studded leather cloaks and other equipment could be recognized. Perhaps the most important site for a study of the whole period is at Vače for it has provided the basis for a chronology of both periods I and II in Slovenia.[18] Sited on a hill-top near iron and copper deposits and an important cross-roads, the fortified settlement was occupied from the eighth to the first century BC and on the south, east and west slopes were the con-temporary cemeteries in which more than one thousand graves have been excavated. The cremation graves were usually older (Vače I 800–600 BC) than the inhumations (Vače II 600–400 BC). Loop-bow and local moulded-bow forms of brooch and metal belts were popular from the first and in Vače II there was a flood of north Italian imports. The famous 'Vače Situla', a bucket with elaborate Etruscan-type funeral scenes on it, was made late in this period.[19] The pottery included 'situlate' and 'fluted-rim' forms. From other cemeteries, such as Novo Mestro and Libni, come fine local bronzework including body armour and helmets,

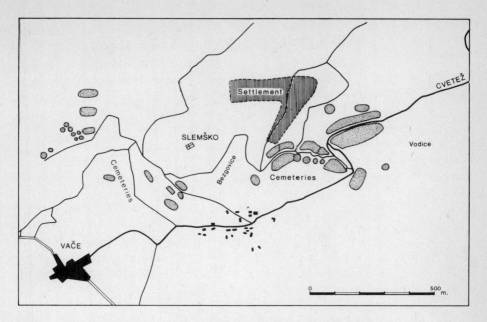

Fig. 65   Plan of Vače showing the settlement and its related cemeteries (after Starè)

important Italian tripods and horse harnesses which suggest 'Thrako-Cimmerian' influence. Much of these riches must have been due to Slovenia being astride the trade routes northeastwards from Venetia, and a Novo Mestro-Stični Horizon (Hallstatt C2 in the Central European terminology) has been recognized as the period of greatest wealth.

The Japodes In much of Croatia and western Bosnia there is a cultural continuity from this period into full historic times and there is little doubt that it belonged to the Illyrian-speaking Japodes, or Ipayges, as the Romans called them. It has been argued that they were already established here in the Bronze Age, but there are certainly many Central European traits in their culture and some movement into the area at the beginning of this period seems likely.[20] Settlements were concentrated in the basins of the Rivers Kupa and Una, and on the great Lika intermontane valley. In the Kupa Valley, near extensive iron deposits, the cemetery at Vinicia first came into use in the sixth century with the same mixed rites as the Slovenian cemeteries, but with metal objects that link it with the Lika and Una Basins. In the Lika Basin there are many hill-

Fig. 66

forts and cemeteries of which Prozor and Kompolje respectively are good examples.[21] The metal objects found show strong connections with central Dalmatia and with eastern central Italy, the trade route from them coming through the Knin Pass; Greek objects are rare. In the Una Valley similar sites and material are found and here, too, there are rich copper and iron deposits which, from the evidence at Sehovic, were being exploited.[22] At Ripac (near Bihac) was one of a number of riverside settlements which flourished in this period. It was built on oak piles between two islands in the River Una and the domestic evidence, which included much organic debris, gives a picture of a well-equipped community working iron, copper, bronze, lead and silver and farming a wide range of animals and plants.[23] Among the cemeteries, Jeserine, where the five hundred and fifty-two cremation and inhumation graves span the period from the sixth to the first century BC, and Ribic, where the graves date mainly from the fifth to the fourth century, are the most important. The wealth of these communities was probably linked with the sixth-century development of Greek trade already mentioned, for at Jeserine the earlier graves show strong central Italian influences, whilst the later have imported Greek pottery and tombstones which may show Greek influence. At Ribic there is less Italian influence, while the strong Greek influence affected the stone-carving of horses and cattle (which stylistically may be the oldest), of a warrior with greaves and helmet, and of a frieze of horsemen. Carvings of women show them wearing long skirts and bodices leaving the right shoulder bare, but these probably belong to Period II.[24] Fortified hill-top settlements are also found here.

The third big inland region in central and eastern Bosnia, Hercegovina and western Serbia consists of the basins of the Rivers Vrbas, Bosna, Drina and Upper Naretva. The evidence suggests that in this period its inhabitants were in contact with the Mediterranean world mainly through the Naretva Valley, and that they were descended from the local Bronze Age peoples.

In Hercegovina there is much evidence of Greek trade from the sixth century onwards and the large cemetery at Gorica contained imported sixth- and fifth-century Greek objects: pottery, a Corinthian-style helmet and personal ornaments. Its native connections were with central Bosnia. Grude, Osanic (Stolac) and a string of hill-forts leading into the interior via the Naretva Valley also belong to this period.[25]

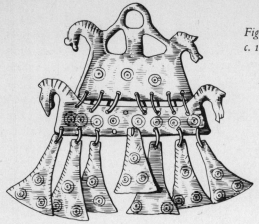

Fig. 66   Bronze pendant (or proton) from Vinicia.
c. 1 : 3

The Glasinac Culture   In Bosnia the dead from a wide region must have been buried in the Glasinac Valley for to them, their ancestors and descendants belong an estimated twenty thousand graves of the tenth-first centuries BC. At least twenty-five groups of tumuli, many of the tumuli forming separate cemeteries of several hundred burials, are known. Of those excavated some 60 per cent were inhumations and the rest cremations, the Iron Age burials continuing to be surrounded by stones or laid on stone pavements in the earlier tradition.[26] In Glasinac III some of the graves contained considerable wealth; for example at Brezje, Tumulus I grave I and Ilijak, Tumulus II, two men each had two iron swords, also a whetstone, bronze buttons, and an amber necklace. Another grave in Tumulus II at Osova had iron spears, a horse bit and harness fittings showing Scythian influence, Greek-type brooches and a pin, and fluted bronze bowls that might show Anatolian influence.[27]

Fig. 67

In three river basins (Vrbas, Bosna and Drina) gold, silver, iron and copper deposits seem to have been worked and the first two exported; this may have been the reason for the sudden increase in wealth. The local metal industry also flourished and new types like the large flat-catchplated 'Glasinac' brooch and the two-shanked pin seem local inventions.

Throughout the region, especially around the Glasinac Valley where thirty are known, fortified single-rampart hill-settlements like Pod and

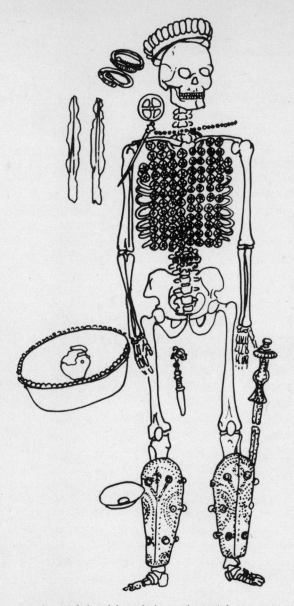

Fig. 67   Male burial from Ilijak, tumulus II (after Hoernes)

Debelo Brdo are found and belong to this and to the succeeding period. Valley settlements like Donja Dolina are also known. The latter, founded in the Late Bronze Age,[28] flourished through this and the next period, and on the bank of the Save, where flooding was likely, the houses were raised on piles to make a series of terraces. Much organic matter survived and shows that the settlement was defended by a box-construction wooden rampart of a type known from Poland to Italy, reinforced with earth and stones. The rectangular two- or three-roomed houses had plank floors and stone reinforced hearths. The animals kept – cattle, sheep and pigs – were identified by dung and bones, and the crops by seeds and pips. Nearby were found inhumation burials in which the deceased had been laid in wooden coffins and wore clothes and jewellery, some of Italian and Greek type. Metal was evidently being worked in the settlement since moulds and slag were found in quantity. There is no doubt that Slovenian, Greek, Italian and possibly Anatolian influences were felt here and this suggests a flourishing long-distance trade.

Fig. 68

Fig. 69

Plate 42

Bosnian influence is also seen in several neighbouring countries; in Romania the Balte Verde group of the Basarabi Culture was much affected by it in the period 650–550 BC and about this time Bosnian forms are also found in Macedonia, Bulgaria and Greece. The double-shanked pin and 'Strbči' brooch were especially widespread. Since these were alien to the Greek tradition and belong to the full historic period in Greece, they are best seen as indicators of peaceful or near-peaceful connections between the regions.[29]

In western Serbia continuity is also suggested by the burial rites, which are similar to those at Glasinac. There is a splendour about those at Atenica which suggests greater social distinctions than have been noticed before; Tumulus II, for example, was 70 metres in diameter and beneath it was a single cremation strewn over a rectangular stone platform five metres square. Nearby but still under the mound were the pyre, the burials of dog, pigs and cattle, a perimeter wall of stones, and four rectangular enclosures. A cart and many objects of gold, iron and bronze had been burnt or buried with the dead.[30] This must be the grave of a person of great consequence.

Figs. 70–72

East of the mountains in northern Serbia and eastern Croatia a different series of influences are apparent. Beyond the reach of Dalmatian trade routes, this area was affected by a succession of south Russian

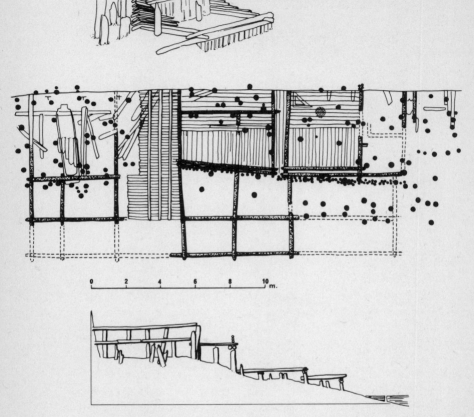

Fig. 68 Isometric projection, plan and section of part of the settlement at Donja Dolina (after Truhelka)

Fig. 69 Female grave from Donja Dolina, with enlargements of the objects found. Objects c. 1 : 4 (after Truhelka)

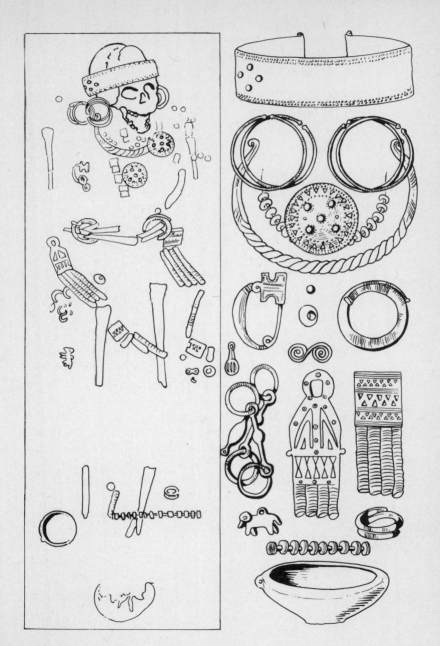

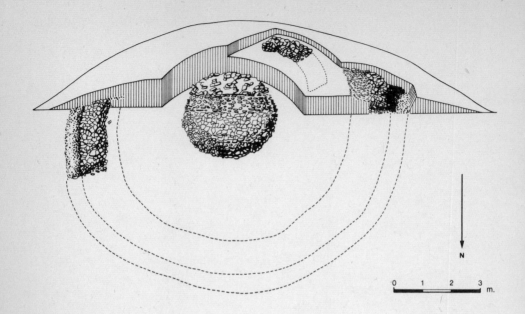

steppe-peoples and by Greek and Anatolian influences coming overland from Macedonia and perhaps even from the Black Sea coasts.

Thrako-Cimmerians The eastern influences began with the horse-riders and drivers still often known by Childe's name of Thrako-Cimmerians. Their characteristic bronze horse harness and equipment mountings belong to the eighth-seventh centuries (Hallstatt B3-C) in Central Europe. Although they do not seem to have penetrated far in Jugoslavia a sheath-mount from Sabac is of south Russian type, and their horse harness comes from Dalja, Barajevo and Rudovci.[31] The finds belong to the earliest local Iron Age, the hoard from Rudovci, for example, containing 'spectacle' safety-pins of kinds fashionable in Slovenia and Croatia in the seventh century. Other metal objects in the region, like the safety-pins from Vinča, suggest Greek models, but some of the earliest iron forms like the socketed iron axes from the Rudnik hoard copy local Late Bronze Age types.

Scythian Influence In the late sixth and early fifth century (the Hallstatt D/La Tène transition in Central European terminology) Scythian influence in the southern Balkans was considerable and traces of it are found in Jugoslavia. The hoard of Kosovo Janjevo, the tri-barbed

Fig. 58

Fig. 70   Schematic section of the excavation of barrow I at Atenica (after Djuknić and Jovanović)

Fig. 71   Plan of barrows I and II at Atenica (after Djuknić and Jovanović)

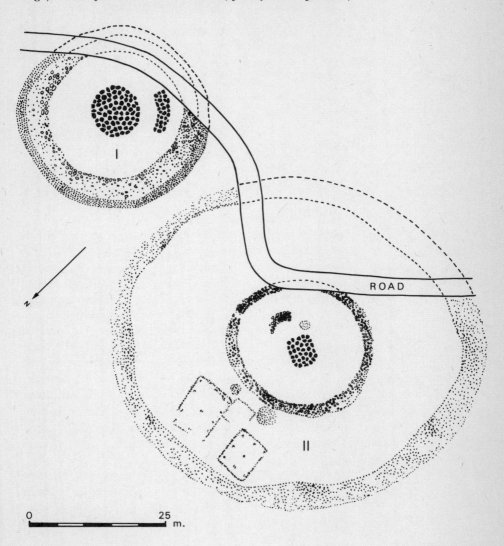

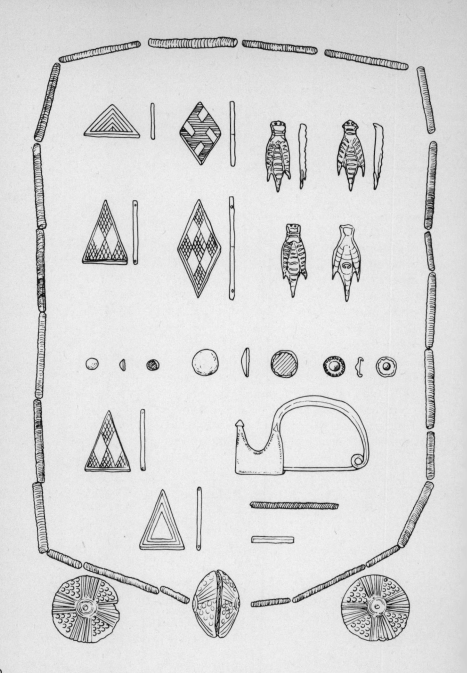

socketed arrow-heads at Hrustovača, Magdalenska Gora, Vače and Ljubljana, and the 'whirligig' ornament from Magdalenska Gora have been held to show their influence, but this may have been transmitted via the Greeks.

The fortified settlements and cemeteries of this period carry on the local Bronze Age traditions for urnfield burial was still practised, and settlements like Zeljesno Doba and Dalja continued to be occupied. The pottery, as at Gornja Stražava, is often plain grey but still included biconic urns. The metal hoards now show close connections with Bosnia and fine moulded long-horned cattle and bird pendants come from Kostolac and Vranovo.

Fig. 73
Plate 41

In southern Serbia and Macedonia, the last inland region to be considered, the first knowledge of iron-using may have come, through connections with Greece, as early as 1000 BC, but it was only after the eighth century that it became common.[32] At this time there was evidence of connections with Bosnia as well as with Greece.

Trebenište Culture In the sixth century BC very distinctive local groups, to which the name Trebenište Culture[33] has been given, evolved. The Greek literary evidence shows that the region was inhabited by Illyrian-speaking tribes, the names of several of them, Dardani, Paeones, Enchelli and Penestae, being known. In the fifth century the hereditary rulers of these tribes were called 'kings' by the Greeks, and some, like the rulers of Greek Macedonia, claimed to be of Greek origin. The cemetery of one such dynasty has been found at Trebenište on the north

Fig. 57

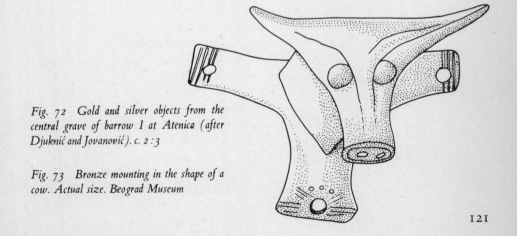

Fig. 72 *Gold and silver objects from the central grave of barrow I at Atenica (after Djuknić and Jovanović). c. 2:3*

Fig. 73 *Bronze mounting in the shape of a cow. Actual size. Beograd Museum*

Plates 47, 48 side of Lake Ochrid.[34] The ten male and three female inhumations belonging to the last quarter of the sixth century were well provided for, some of them wearing sheet-gold death masks, which show the men to have been clean-shaven, and sheet-gold glove and sandal covers. Gold and silver pins and brooches of Greek and Bosnian type and amber and glass beads were common. Also buried with the dead were imported Greek objects, including some in Corinthian styles and a very large (1.5 m. high) bronze krater probably made, like the similar one from Vix in France, in a Chalicidician workshop. Pottery (Black-Figure Ware) from Attica was also imported. A fine drinking-horn which had its rim decorated with gold throws some light on local drinking habits. Many other sites, like Stobi and Radolište, show Greek influence of this period and from Novi Pazar comes a hoard of embossed gold strips perforated for attachment to some organic material, possibly cloth, which has since perished.

These Illyrian-speaking tribes seem to have been pressing upon neighbouring Greeks at least as early as the sixth century BC, and continued to do so during the fifth. This resulted in Greek influence along the land routes into central Jugoslavia being minimal. Not until the successful campaigns of Philip and Alexander of Macedonia in 339–335 BC was the frontier quiet and trade to the north considerable.

EARLY IRON AGE II (*c.* 350–11 BC)

After 400 BC Jugoslavia begins to emerge into the light of history; the armies of more sophisticated neighbours marched through some regions, traders and explorers visited the rest, and then the empires of the Mediterranean began to control and annexe.

Reaction to these changes was very varied in different parts of Jugoslavia; some tribes, like the Veneti, accepted the new conditions, throve on them, and were incorporated as allies and partners; others, like the Japodes, turned to raiding their richer neighbours and were conquered by force.

Several general tendencies can be observed. In the frontier zones on the west and south, urban civilization began to develop and a series of towns, many of them to achieve Roman recognition, were founded in Slovenia, Dalmatia and Macedonia. Elsewhere the tribal pattern of organization centred on fortified settlements continued but there was, as elsewhere in Europe at this time, a tendency towards larger and stronger confederations. Military confederations of almost all of the mountain tribes may in fact have taken place in Croatia and Bosnia in 34 BC and AD 6. These great united attempts to counter the menace of Rome were similar to that led by Vercingetorix in France.

Since a number of events and finds can be given absolute dates, a local subdivision of the period can be recognized both north and south of the mountains in the middle of the second century.

The Southern Frontier Zone   In the early fourth century the most northerly Greek-speaking regions of Macedonia and Epirus were hard put to it to hold their own against their Illyrian-speaking neighbours in Jugoslavia and Albania. In 360 BC, for example, Bardylis, ruler of the Lyncus region beside Lake Ohrid, was powerful enough to overrun much of Greek Macedonia, and at the time of his defeat a few years later could muster more than 10,000 men. After his successor's defeat, much of Jugoslav Macedonia passed into Alexander the Great's empire and the first known town in the region, Aerachia Lynci, was founded. From this time on, the history of the region was to be incorporated in first the Macedonian and then the Roman Empire. The archaeological evidence shows increasing Greek influence and there was much importing of pottery, metalwork, glass, coins, etc. Sites which show this development well are Stobi, Radolište and Beravči near Bitolj, the latter a cemetery showing fourth-century connections in Macedonia and Thrace (the Chalcide). Demir Kapija near Skopje may have been a Greek colony from the late fifth century onwards and the grave of an Athenian of that date has been found there.[35]

Plate 52

The northern expeditions by Philip and Alexander in 346–343 and 335 BC penetrated far into Serbia and provide evidence of more tribes. In the Morava Valley were the Dardani, the name of one of their rulers, Pluvatus, being recorded; east of the Morava and stretching into Bulgaria were the Triballi, and west of it and stretching into Montenegro the Autariatai; all were said to be Illyrian-speaking. Finds of coins, metal and pottery objects from this period show increasing Greek penetration of the Middle Danube Basin, but objects of Bosnian type continue to be fashionable. Josanička Banja in the Morava Basin, and further north, Zeljezno Doba and Dalja in the Save Valley show in their metal and pottery styles that the older local traditions survived.

About 300 BC much of northern Serbia was occupied by the Celtic-speaking Scordisci, who brought with them a version of the Central European La Tène Culture; they are discussed on page 128.

The Western Frontier Zone On the Dalmatian coast before 375 BC, Greek colonies with the possible exception of the precocious settlement on Korčula (p. 107) had not been founded further north than at Durazzo in Albania; Dalmatia had therefore remained outside the Greek world. This strange isolation was broken by invasion from Sicily. In 385 BC, Dionysus the Elder, ruler of Syracuse, as part of a complicated foreign policy, established colonies on the island of Hvar (then called Pharos) and on Viš (then called Issa). If a first-century BC source is to be believed, there was also some settlement, or reinforcement, of earlier trading stations on Brač.[36] Besides being a political move to break the trade monopoly of Corinth and her colonies, the settlements may well have been placed off the mouth of the River Naretva to control the trade with the interior.

These settlements flourished through the troubled years of the fourth and early third centuries. Little archaeological detail from most of them is yet known, but a colony on Viš has been located at Prirovo.[37] The site chosen, a bay protected by a peninsula, has strong similarities to the mother-town of Syracuse and the town was a walled rectangle some 200 metres long with a regular pattern of streets inside and extensive cemeteries nearby. From the latter has come much imported south Italian pottery of the mid-fourth century. Several towns including Issa, Pharos and the as yet unlocated Heraclea Illyrici, struck their own coins, often over-stamped, from the fourth to the second century.[38] Those of Issa (Viš) bore at first the head of Ionas, son of Adrias, the eponymous hero of the region who may have been a pre-Greek ruler on Viš, and also grapes and goats. A fine hoard of them came from Stari Grad (perhaps the ancient city of Pharos) on Hvar. Pottery and terracotta statuettes of this period also come from Vičja Luka and Blatno on Korčula whilst from Lumbaria came an important fourth century inscription.

On the mainland, the immediate coastal plain seems to have been controlled from Cape Ploča, in the Split region, where Solin was one of the most northerly settlements, through Epetion near the mouth of the Cetina, and Narona at the mouth of the Naretva to Kotor, Budva, and beyond. The cremation cemetery at Budva (Bouthoe) was especially rich

Plates 53, 54

in imported Greek pottery, bronzes and gold and silver jewellery, although the latter includes copies of Bosnian types. Further north the colonies gradually extended their influence over the coastlands. There are for example mentions of wars with the Iadertini (the people of Zadar) in central Dalmatia. Sites like Podgradje (Asseria) and Babska in that region have rich material of this period including graceful silver 'Liburnian' brooches with leaf terminals to the catch-plate.

Greek influence in the interior also increased. There are many imports, including coins, at Jeserine and Sanskimost in the Una and Sana Valleys, at Gorica and Medum (Podgorica) in the Naretva Basin, and further inland at Strbči, and Osovo. The literary references to Greek (Thasian and Chiot) pottery being found in the River Naretva and to exports of salt, cattle, slaves, horses and fowls may date to this time, but otherwise there is little indication of the nature of the trade carried on. It is likely that silver and perhaps hides were exported. It was presumably this trade which required the use of the large numbers of coins which are found in Bosnia and Hercegovina.

The middle of the third century was a time of much local fighting. A Dalmatian ruler, Demetrius of Pharos, established control over Corfu far to the south, but at the same period the Greeks on Viš were petitioning Rome for help against the natives. There was much raiding of Italian and Greek merchant ships, the pirate centre being at Scodra (Scutari) in Albania.

The Northern Frontier Zone In western Slovenia the Veneti probably controlled the western slopes of the Julian Alps and Istria as far as the River Axus in the fourth as they did in the second century BC. Their existence during those centuries was threatened by the presence of warlike Celtic-speaking peoples to the north and west.

Fig. 57

The conquest of the Po Valley by Celtic-speaking Gauls between 600 and 400 BC left the Veneti independent but isolated, for Celtic-speaking tribes were also in occupation of the mountain valleys to the north and east. The finds from these valleys, for example at Bled (Prištava), suggest that commercial connections with the Veneti were maintained and, as a result of the contacts, Venetian metalwork styles became much affected by Alpine (La Tène) fashions. At cemeteries like Idrja (Bača) and Sv. Skočijan, new types of safety-pin brooches, including penannular ones, were common.

In Istria numerous fortified settlements testifying to the uncertainty of the times, and settlements like Nezakcij and Pula in the extreme south, the safest region, flourished. Sea connections were maintained with Italy and Greece and at Nezakcij (Nezactium) some of the large stone statues already mentioned may date to this time.[39]

During the Romano-Gaulish (225–220 BC) and Romano-Carthaginian (218–202 BC) wars the Veneti were allies of Rome and after 202 BC their position was secure. Although their main area of urbanisation (where more than fifty towns were later reported) lay in Italy, Istria and western Slovenia benefited from that security. The establishment of a Roman colony at Aguileia close to the present Jugoslav frontier in 184 BC merely continued the existing process of unification.

The Save and Drave Basins and the Celtic Invasions By the fifth century BC the restless Celtic-speaking tribes in Central Europe had developed, from a mixture of indigenous, Mediterranean and East European traits, an original and artistic cultural tradition usually named 'La Tène'. Some of these tribes, who migrated to the south-east along the Save and Drave Valleys, had penetrated into the Middle Danube Basin by the early fourth century. In 335 BC some of their envoys journeyed into Romania to meet Alexander the Great and perhaps to spy out the land, for within a generation they had arrived there in force and by 279 BC their war-bands in Macedonia had killed one of Alexander's successors. In the following centuries many parts of Jugoslavia were under pressure from Celtic invaders and much of Slovenia, Croatia and Serbia was conquered and occupied by them. The indigenous inhabitants held their own in the mountains but even here there was considerable mixing and much adoption of La Tène fashions.

In the north, in the Upper Drave and Save Basins, a number of tribes were known in the first century BC as *Pannonians*, and these, from their archaeological remains, were a culturally mixed group with many Central European 'La Tène' customs and fashions. Many of the earlier cemeteries and fortified settlements, however, continued to be used through the period. Settlement was concentrated, as before, westwards from Ljubljana and there are many finds from the Celj and Maribor areas. New cemeteries like Mehovo Formen, Drejina Vas and Kostreonica are found, whilst older ones like Vače, Mokronog and Podzemelj remained in use. Settlements like Ulaka contain pedestal

Fig. 74

126

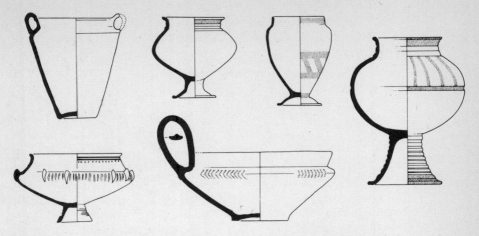

Fig. 74 Vače; pottery from the cemeteries of periods II and III, showing pedestal forms. c. 1 : 6 (after Starè)

wheel-made pottery and much ironwork including door-keys, hoes and plough-shares. Defended hill-top settlements, some of great size as at Vače (Period III 400–100 BC) are common. The metalwork includes fine La Tène brooches and the typical curvilinear La Tène ornamental motifs were popular.[40] Coins, many of Norican (south Austrian) type, were coming into use throughout the region, and have been found on at least twenty sites. Trade connections with northern Italy and the Veneti remained strong and are mentioned in the literary evidence. For example, the envoys from Celtic-speaking tribes who visited Alexander the Great had come from somewhere in the north of the Middle Danube Basin, perhaps from Slovenia, where they had been in contact with the Veneti. This is also mentioned by Pliny, the fourth-century historian, who refers to the Veneti carrying amber from Pannonia (which included the Drave Valley in Slovenia) to Italy.

Fig. 65

With the founding of the Roman colony at Aquileia a stable frontier in the Julian Alps was established and Roman interference beyond it, in the interests of a peaceful frontier, began to report tribes like the Latobici in the Kupa Valley and the Serretes beyond. Other Celtic, or mixed Celtic-Illyrian groups, now occupied the whole of the Lower Drave and Save Valleys in Croatia and Serbia.

The number and distribution of cemeteries, settlements and hill-forts suggest a considerable population at this time. At Sisak on the junction of the Kupa and Save, for example, was the famous fortress of Segesta, first seen by a Roman punitive expedition in 146 BC, but uncaptured until 35 BC. From it and other sites, like Metrovice, Dolni Lanume, Kupinovo, Sotin, Dalja and Zeljezno Doba came wheel-turned burnished pottery with moulded ornament and strap handles. The iron-work included fine weapons: long spike-tanged swords in sheaths decorated in the curvilinear 'Sword' Style,[41] long and short socketed spears and rectangular shield-bosses. Most of the ornaments were of bronze and silver and included brooches (types I and II of the Central European La Tène typology) with enamel inlay, bracelets and rings. Locally-made coins copying Greek types, as at Ribniacka, are wide-spread.

The Scordisci The largest and most famous tribe was in northern Serbia, and was probably centred near, but south of, the junction of the Rivers Danube, Tiza and Morava. These were the Scordisci, who were power-ful over a wide area for several centuries.[42] The citadel of Beograd, the Kalimagdan, known to the Romans by the Celtic name of Singidunum, was doubtless theirs as was the nearby cremation cemetery of Rospi Čuprija. At Židovar, near Bela Crkva, a hill settlement of this period has been excavated. Defended by a stone wall, which was perhaps strengthened by transverse timbers, it consisted of a number of small huts set over depressions in the ground. The huts had doors opened by iron keys and from the lack of other debris were probably built of wood and thatched. A circular enclosure containing small pits has been identified as a shrine.[43] Here and elsewhere there was fine wheel-turned pottery with cordon, groove and painted ornament. Amongst their metalwork, the bronze and silver serpent-terminaled bracelets and the brooches (in styles La Tène I-III) were especially fine.

Fig. 75

Plate 40

The Mountains of the Interior Although the mountains of Croatia, Bosnia-Hercegovina and Montenegro were not permanently occupied by Celts, Greeks or Romans before 35 BC, raids, punitive expeditions and at times peaceful amalgamations brought changes. Tribes like the Japodes, Pesitates and Autoriates, however, continued to survive and even flourish through the period.

In the north the Japodes continued to live in the Kupa, Una and Lika Basins.[44] In the Kupa Valley the cremations and inhumations, some beneath tumuli, of the cemetery at Vinicia largely belong to this

Fig. 75   Pottery from Židovar (after Gavela)

period. With the dead were buried wheel-turned pedestal-urns, some with black-and-white friezes of Venetic style, La Tène-type brooches (the Central European division into types I, II and III does not seem to apply here), distinctive scabbard-mounts and bronze-studded belts of a type long popular in Slovenia. There were many similarities with the objects found in the Lika and Una Valleys, especially at Jeserine. In the valley of the Upper Una, too, there were hill-forts, lowland settle-ments and cemeteries. The cemetery at Jeserine (p. 112) continued in use through the period; the graves contained many imported Greek and south Italian objects, one vase having a third-century BC inscription in the Latin alphabet. The metalwork included local variants of La Tène brooches, many objects of east Bosnian (Glasinac) type and enduring local forms. Especially interesting are the numerous amber necklaces, the ornaments with horse-head terminals and the brooches with cross-bow springs. Nearby at Bihac, where there was also much amber, there were sculptured tombstones of the fourth-third centuries with geometric patterns showing strong Roman influence and another Latin alphabet inscription. In the Sana Valley, where the *Mezeri* tribe was to be found in the first century BC, south Italian and Greek objects of the fourth-third centuries were found at Sanskimost. With them were spectacle brooches and lug adzes which showed the conservative tastes of the tribesmen. Throughout the region hill-forts are common and multivallate ones are found, some, like Gradac, being much modified over several centuries.

Plate 43

Further south in Bosnia, southern Serbia and Montenegro the Daesitiates and Pirustae can be recognized as the peoples who continued to bury their dead in the Glasinac cemeteries and to use the fortified settlements of the Vrbas, Bosna and Drina Basins. In the Bosna Valley the long-established settlements of Debelo Brdo and Donja Dolina continued in Roman times. At Donja Dolina La Tène type brooches were found with coins which, like many Celtic ones in Central Europe, imitated those used in Macedonia in the reign of Philip II, but in the Bosna Valley generally there was a notable absence of 'Celtic' coins. At Glasinac (Period V) there were very few La Tène-style objects but a very wide variety of local forms. Rich graves, like those from Zagradge tumulus III, Rusanice tumulus XLI and Ilijak tumulus XV, continue to be found and it has been argued that these and similar finds, including armour from Čitluci, indicate an aristocratic class.

In the Vrbas Basin the iron mines of Majdar and Sinjokovo (Jaijce) seem to have been in use at this time.[45]

Greek imports come from many Bosnian sites, for example, Mahrevice, Osovo and Strbči. The last site has given its name to a type of silver brooch which was popular further south in Macedonia.

In Hercegovina and Montenegro, connections with the coastal Greek colonies were strong and the names and the troubled histories of several tribes are known. That of the Ardiei may be given as an example; they appeared on the Adriatic coast in the River Naro region between 500 and 400 BC, were attacked by Celts in 370 BC and moved inland. Defeated there by Illyrians they moved back to the coast where they fought the Romans until 167 BC. When badly defeated they moved to the Kotor region and were finally dispersed in 135 BC.[46] Settlements and cemeteries, as at Gorica, Medak and Melin, indicate a considerable population and much Greek and Italian trade. Duvno (Gradina kod Gaja) in southwestern Bosnia might well be the ancient Delminium and belong to this time.[47] One of the most southerly sites, Momišić in Montenegro, was still strongly non-Greek in the third century BC.

The Coming of the Romans Roman relationships with Jugoslavia developed from two series of events: the earlier, in the southern Adriatic, involved the Punic and Macedonian wars of the third and second centuries; the later, in the northern Adriatic, the Roman conquest of the Gaulish tribes of the Po Valley in the second century BC.[48]

Having completed their conquest of the east coast of Italy in 244 BC, the Romans were soon involved in Dalmatian affairs. Appeals from the Greeks of Viš and Corfu for help against the local tribes, conveniently described as pirates, and the maltreatment of a Roman embassy sent to a queen-regent in Albania, resulted in a successful punitive campaign in 229 BC. Demetrius (p. 125) was left as a Roman ally with control over an unspecified area of coastland, but ten years later another campaign deposed him, and from then on 'the kingdom of Illyria', as the southern Jugoslav and Albanian coast was called, remained in close relationship with Rome. The Roman-Macedonian wars (214–148 BC) meant that Roman armies and fleets were frequently in Illyria and alliances were made with some of the inland peoples. In 167 BC a reorganization of the area left three states in existence but when Macedonia became a Roman province after 148 BC, Illyria was attached to it. Archaeological evidence of these developments includes imports of Italian pottery, coin series, especially from Kotor (Rhizon) and Hvar, and also the use of the Latin script for Illyrian inscriptions. The Delmatae tribe was the main opponent of any extension of Roman influence at this period and developed a series of stone-walled hill-forts with artificially heightened strong points which anticipate the medieval motte-and-bailey castle.[49]

Fig. 76

Further north the wars of the Romans against the Gaulish tribes in the Po Valley were won by 200 BC and the Veneti, as Roman allies, were left secure. From this time onwards the Venetic lands were regarded as part of metropolitan Italy, the boundaries after 184 BC being the Julian Alps and the River Axus in south Istria. In spite of raids by Celtic and Illyrian neighbours and threats of invasion by the Germanic Cimbri, the whole region flourished and Trieste (Tergeste), Pula and other cities developed.

The mountainous interior of Jugoslavia became a problem to the Romans only after they had accepted the role of frontier guardians in Macedonia, Dalmatia and Venetia. From about 180 BC onwards a

Fig. 76   Diagramatic plans of fortified settlements in Dalmatia (after Wilkes)

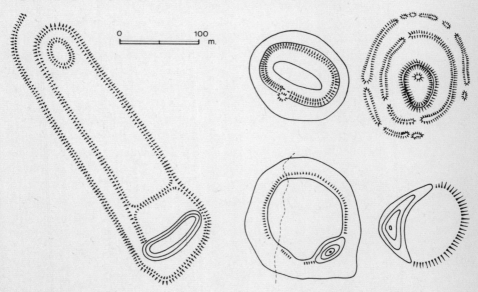

series of punitive expeditions were mounted, usually as a punishment for raiding.

By 10 BC all Jugoslavia, with the exception of part of Serbia north of the Danube, was within the Roman Empire, and the previous one hundred and fifty years shows a pattern of local resistance which much resembled that of the Gauls in France. That the resistance in Jugoslavia was more successful and more protracted was due to the mountainous central regions which then, as in our own lifetime, made occupation by an enemy difficult. It says much for the efficiency of Roman soldiers and diplomats that they succeeded where other later and better-equipped invaders failed.

The coastal areas were steadily if unsystematically absorbed. In the early first century organizations of Roman citizens are mentioned at Salona (Solin near Split) which was captured in *c.* 76 BC, at Epidauram (near Dubrovnik) and at Narona; there were also prosperous towns from Zadar to Budva and on the islands.[50] Podgradje kod Benkovac (Asseria)

Fig. 77

illustrates their sophistication. A hill-top of some 17,500 sq. metres was enclosed by a mortared stone wall pierced by three gates, and on its weakest side was reinforced by four square external towers. The coin hoards of this period are particularly interesting although only one Illyrian tribe, the Daorsii, are known to have minted their own. Important hoards were buried between 90 and 80 BC at Morter (Šibenik), Dolni Unac and Mazun; the last had more than eight hundred coins including many minted in Sicily, Italy, Carthage and Egypt.[51] Many of the graves at Budva, where the dead of a rich Hellenistic community were buried, also date from this time. The years between 60 and 35 BC were full of turmoil, Salona being at one time besieged by Delmataean tribesmen, and Roman relief expeditions meeting with varied success. In 35 BC the whole area was conquered by a combined land and sea drive commanded by Octavianus, the young Augustus Caesar.[52]

Plate 50

In the interior a series of Roman raids also took place, but in between them there seems to have been a steady increase in Mediterranean influence. In the south, the imported Greek marble statue from Bitolj, the gold jewellery from Djevajalja and fine pottery and figurines at Olbia and Demir Kapija show how a local taste for Hellenistic forms had developed. Further north in Serbia at Kladova and Brestovik simple grey wheel-made pottery and metal objects of late La Tène style carry on

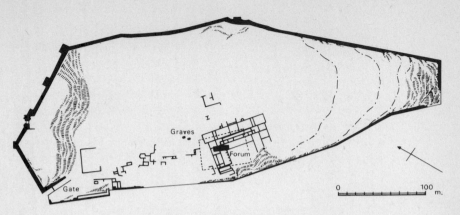

Fig. 77   Plan of Podgradje kod Benkovac, Asseria (after Suić)

the traditions of the previous period and still show connections with
Central Europe. Here the spear-heads are very large with long narrow
sockets, the sword-sheaths have 'strangulated' shapes and the brooches
have big springs and elaborate bows. At sites like Paraćin the pottery
styles are close to the 'Dacian' forms in Romania.[53]

In Croatia, Bosnia, Hercegovina and Montenegro there is no evidence
that any attempt was made to conquer the mountain tribes, other than
the Delmatae, before 35 BC, but coins of the Roman Republic are found
across the country with concentrations in Slovenia and Croatia. In
Octavianus' description to the Senate of his campaign of 35 BC he listed
twenty-one conquered tribes; one group in Hercegovina and Montenegro
was first subdued and then a series of northern tribes, including the
Japodes of Croatia. The latter were attacked from the south and
Octavianus took, first, the capital (?Prozor) which was undefended,
and then a large hill-fort (?Metulum near Josipdol) which enclosed two
hill-tops with a palisade and was defended by three thousand men. A
march through the Kupa Valley finally brought Octavianus to the Sava
Valley where Segesta (Sisak) was taken.

In spite of forts and an army of occupation of fifteen thousand men, a
confederation of the inland tribes revolted the next year and, even after
a defeat at Peplin (probably Premona near Šibenik), continued to fight
for many months. Versus and Testimus, their leaders, should rank with
Vercingetorix and Caractacus among the earliest and ablest organisers
of resistance movements in Europe.

The last part of Jugoslavia to be conquered lay between the Rivers Save and Drave, its Celtic-speaking inhabitants being known as Pannonians. In AD 6 they and some of the tribes of the province of Illyricum revolted, led by Bato, chief of the Daesitiates (central Bosnia). When this revolt was crushed in three campaigns by Tiberius, the future emperor, the frontier was advanced beyond the Drave.

For the first time the whole of the region now lay in the hands of one ruler.

Notes on the Text

ABBREVIATIONS

AFEQ   *Bulletin de l'Association Française, Études Quatenaire*

AJA   *American Journal of Archaeology, Princeton*

Arch Iug   *Arheologica Iugoslavica, Beograd*

Arh Rad   *Arheološki Radovi e Rasprave (Jugoslav Academy), Zagreb*

AV   *Arheološki Vjestnik (Slovene Academy), Ljubljana*

BASPR   *Bulletin of the American School for Prehistoric Research, Cambridge (USA)*

BJ   *Bonner Jahrbücher, Bonn*

Bul Sc Yug   *Bulletin Scientifique Yougoslavienne,*

BPI   *Bulletino di Paletnologia Italiana, Parma*

BRGK   *Bericht der Römisch Germanischen Kommission, Frankfurt am Main*

BSA   *Annual of the British School of Archaeology at Athens, London*

BSPF   *Bulletin de la Societé préhistorique française, Le Mans*

CBI   *Godišnjak, Centar za Balkanološka ispitivanja, Sarajevo*

F und F   *Forschungen und Forschritte, Berlin*

GZMS   *Glasnik Zemalskog Muzeja Sarajevu, Sarajevo*

MAGW   *Mitteilungen der Anthropologischen Gesellschaften, Vienna*

OA   *Opuscula Arheologica, Zagreb*

Porčila   *Poročila o Raznisk neo- e eneo-lit Sloveniji, Ljubljana*

PPS   *Proceedings of the Prehistoric Society, Cambridge (England)*

PZ   *Prähistorische Zeitschrift, Berlin*

Raz/Dis   *Raz/Dissertationes (Slovene Academy), Ljubljana*

Rad Jug   *Rad (Jugoslav Academy), Zagreb*

Starinar   *Starinar (Serbian Academy), Beograd*

VAHD   *Vjesnik za arheologiju i istorijuna Dalmatinsku, Split*

Vi Arh Hv   *Vjesnik za Arhiologiju Hrvatcke Zagreb*

VjAMZ   *Vjesnik Arheološki Muzej u Zagrebu, Zagreb*

WMBH   *Wissenschaftliche Mitteilungen aus Bosnien und der Hercegovina, Sarajevo*

ZA   *Ziva Anticha, Skoplje*

ZFF   *Zbornik Filozofske Fakultete Ljubljana*

ZMS   *Zbornik Matica Srpska, Beograd*

Entries marked with an asterik are in English

CHAPTER I

1 Benac. A., *BRGK*, 40, 1962, 1–3; *Valoch, K., *Current Anthropology*, 9.5, 1968; Maudit, J., *BSPF*, 47, 1946.

2 *Butzer, K., *Environment and Archaeology*, London, 1965, 276.

3 *Higgs, E. and Vita-Finzi, C., *PPS*. XXXII, 1966 and XXXIII, 1967.

4 Marković-Marjanović, J., *AFEQ* VII, 1969, and *Starinar NS* VII-VIII, 1965.

5 Vuković, S., *AV*, XVIII, 1967, and *Valoch, K., op. cit.

6 Basler, D., Brunnacker, K. and Malez, M., *GZMS*, XI-XII, 1966–7.

7 Brodar, M., *F und F.*, 30, 1956.

8 Gorjanović-Kramberger, K., Malez, M., *Acta Geologica* I, Zagreb, 1956. *MAGW* XXX, 1902 and XXXII, 1904. For English Summary see *MacAlister, R., *A Text-book of European Archaeology*, Vol. I, Cambridge, 1921.

9 *Day, M., *Guide to Fossil Man*, London, 1965. Zivanović, K., *Starinar* XV-XVI, 1964–5.

10 Basler, D., *GZMS*, XVIII, 1963. Malez, M., *Paleontologia Jugoslavia*, 1, 1958 and *Bul Sc Yug.* T7N3, 1962 and *AV* XVIII, 1967.

11 Brodar, M., *F und F* 30, 1956. *Atti VI Cong. Int. della Sc. Pre e Protistoriche,* Rome 1962.

12 Serčelj, A., Dissertations Acad. Scient. Art. Slovenica (Class IV), 1963, and *Raz/Dis.* IX, 1966.

13 Marković-Marjanović, J. Janeković, G., Brunnacker, K., *AFEQ,* 1969.

14 *Valoch, K., op. cit.

15 As suggested by *Higgs, E., for Northern Greece, *PPS NS* XXXII, 1966 and XXXIII, 1967.
Brodar, M., *Festshrift für Zotz,* Berlin, 1960.

16 Osole, F., *Arheološki Pregled* 2, 1960 and *AV* XVII, 1966.

17 Brodar, M., *Quarter* I, 1938. Gavela, B., *Starinar* XIX, 1958.

18 Garašanin, M., *Germania* 46.2 and *WMBH* II, 1894.

19 Graziosi, P., *BSPF* 55, 1951, Čečuk, B., in *Adriatica: praehistorica et antiqua* (ed. Miro-

savljević, V. et al) Zagreb, forthcoming.

20 Brodar, M., and Benac, A., *GZMS*, 13, 1956.

21 Bruckner, K., *Arch. Iug.,* VII, 1966.

22 Radmilli, A., *Atti VII Riunione scient. Inst. Ital. Pre- and Protoistoria* 39, 1963.

23 *Srejović, D., *Arch. Iug.* VII, 1966 and *Lepenski Vir,* Beograd, 1968; *Nandris, J., *Science Journal,* 1968, 64. *Tringham, R., in *Studies in Ancient Europe* (ed. Coles, J. and Simpson, D.) Leicester, 1968.

CHAPTER II

1 For example in *Weinberg, S., *The Stone Age in the Aegean,* Cambridge, 1965, or *Berciu, D., *Romania,* London, 1967, Rodden, W., *PPS* XXVIII, 1962.

2 Milojčić, V., *Germania* 38, 1960, and *BSA*, XLIV, 1949.

3 *Tringham, R. op. cit.

4 Garašanin, D., *Staracevačka Kultura,* Ljubljana, 1954. *Antiquity,* XXXV, 1961.
Galović, R., *Die Starčevo Kultur in Jugoslavien,* Beograd, 1968 and *BRGK* 43.4, 1963. Bruckner, B. in *Proc. VI. Kongress Arh. Jugoslavije,* Beograd, 1964.
*Renfrew, C., *The Arts of the First Farmers,* Sheffield, 1969. and Bregant, T., *Ornamentika na Neolitski Keramiki v Jugoslavij'* Ljubljana, 1968. *Georgiev, F., in *L'Europe à la Fin de l'Age de la Pierre,* (Soudsky, B., and Plesova, E. eds.) Prague, 1961.
Dimitrejević, s., in *Simpozij Neolit i eneolit u Slavoniji,* Vukovar, 1969.

5 This seems particularly true of the Körös variant. See *Tringham R., op. cit.

6 Glišić, J., in *Les Régions Centrales des Balkans à l'Epoque Neolithique* (ed. Trifunović, L.) Beograd, 1968.

Bruckner, B., Neolit. i Vojvodini, *Arch. Dissert. V.,* Beograd-Novi Sad, 1968.

7 *Letica, Z., *Archaeology* 17, 1964. *Galović, B., *Ill. Lond. News* 254, (1969), 28.

8 Garašanin, D., (see note 4) and *Germania* 39, 1961.

9 Neustupny, E., *Slovenska Archaeologia* XIV, 1968, *Chronologies in Old World Archaeology.* Ehrich, R. (ed.) 1965; for general chronology see pp. 403–458.
*Quitta, H., *Antiquity,* XLI, 1967.
Garašanin, M., *Germania* 39, 1961; *Antiquity,* XXXV, 1961.

10 *Renfrew, C., *et al. BSA.* 60, 1965. *Nandris, J., *Man* 5 No. 2. 1970.

11 Čović, B., *BZMS* 15/6, 1960–61. Benac, A. *BRGK* 42, 1962.

12 Batović, Š., *Diadora* I, 1959 and II, 1962. *Stariji neolit u Dalmaciji,* Zadar, 1966. Mirosavljević, V., *Arh. Rad.* II, 1962.

13 Garašanin, M., *Hronologia Vinčanske Gruppe,* Ljubljana 1951 and Popović, V., *Revue Archeologique* II, 1965, favour a short chronology but here the C-14 dates are accepted.

14 Todorović, J. and Cermanović, A., *Banjica, Siedlung der Vinča-Gruppe,* Beograd, 1961. Benac, A., *Arch. Iug* 3, 1959.

15 *Sandars, N., *Prehistoric Art,* London, 1968. *Mellaart, J., *Antiquity* XXXIV, 1960. He suggests that the Antolian connections were with Haçilar rather than Troy.

16 Korošec, J., *Neolitska naseobina u Danilu Bitinju,* Zagreb, 1959. *Danilo i danilska Kultura,* Ljubljana, 1964.
Batović, Š., in *Adriatic: praehistorica et antiqua* (ed. Mirosavljević, V., et al). Zagreb, forthcoming.

17 *Bray, W., *Antiquity* XL, 1966. Actual sherds of Danilo ware are claimed at Ripoli in Italy.

18 Garašanin, M., *BRGK* 39, 1958. Benac, A., *GZMS* XX, 1965.

19 *Galović, R., *AJA* 70, 1966 and *Predionica-Priština,* 1959.

20 Korošec, J., *Lengyel Kult. i Bosnia, Srym e Slovenije,* Ljubljana, 1957.

21 Radimsky, W. and Hoernes, M., *Die Neolit. Station von Butmir,* Vienna, 1895–8, for English summary see *Munro, R., *Travels in Bosnia and Herzegovina,* London, 1890.

22 Benac, A., *Neolitsko naselje Nebo i problem Butmirske Kulture,* Ljubljana 1952, also *GZMS* XX, 1965, and *BRGK* 42, 1961.

23 Korošec, J. (note 16), Bray W. (note 17), Javonić, J., *Starinar* XI, 1960.

24 Battaglia, R., *BPI,* 1958–9.

25 *Novak, G., *Prehistoric Hvar,* Zagreb, 1955 and *Arch. Iug.* III, 1959; Stipčević, A., *Enc. Likimjel,* 1962.

26 Korošec, J., *AV* III/4, 1960, and *Poročila* II, 1963–4; Stalio, B., in *Les Régions Centrales des Balkans dans l'Epoque néolithique* (ed. Trifunović, L.) Beograd, 1968.

27 Jovanović, B., *Arch. Iug. V,* 1964.
*Munro, R., *Lake Dwellings of Europe,* London, 1890.

28 *Barfield, L., Ph.D. dissertation, Cambridge University Library, 1968, and Battaglio, R., *BPI* (special volume on Venezia Guilia) 1958–9.

29 *Childe, V., *Danube in Prehistory,* Cambridge, 1959, and *The Dawn of European Civilisation,* Chapter 6, London, 1956.

CHAPTER III

1 Passek, T. in *L'Europe à la Fin de l'Age de la Pierre,* (Soudsky, B, and Plesova, E. eds), Prague 1961.
*Renfrew, C. *PPS* XXXV, 1969.

Jugoslavia

2 *Mellaart, J., *Antiquity* XXXIV, 1960. *Garašanin, M., *Antiquity* XXXV, 1961 and *Revue des Études Sud-est Européenes* 1.5, 1965. Popović, V., *Arch Iug.* VI, 1965. Trbuhović, L., *Problem porekla i datovanja bronzanog dobo u Srbiji*, Beograd, 1958. Jananović, B., *Arch. Iug.* V, 1964 and *Starinar* XVII, 1966.

3 Garašanin, D., *Katalog Metal Beograd: I*, Beograd, 1954.

4 Todorović, J., *Arch. Iug.* IV 1963 and *GZMS* XXXVI, 1961.

5 Dimitrejević, S., *Arh. Rad. JAZU* II, 1962.

6 *Hencken, H., *American Anthropological Association* 57, 6. pt. 3, 1955.

7 Schmidt, R., *Die Burg Vučedol*, Zagreb, 1945; Tasić, N., in *Simposij: Neolit a Eneolit u Slavoniji*, Vukuvar, 1969.

8 Garašanin, M., *Germania* XXXV, 1957 and *BRGK* 39.1, 1958.

9 *Tasić, N., *Arch. Iug.* VII, 1966. Benac, A., *GZMS* XVII and XVIII, 1962, 63.

10 Dimitrejević, S., (*op cit.*)

11 Vinski-Gasparini, K., *Vj Arh Hv* LVI-IX, 1954-7.

12 Benac, A., *BRGK* 42, 1962.

13 Deschmann, A., *MAGW* VIII, 1876. Bregant, T., in *Procilo o Raziskovanjci neolita in Eneoleta v Sloveniji*, Ljubljana, 1964. Dimitrejević, S., *Arch. Iug.* VIII, 1967. *Munro, R. *Lake Dwellings of Europe*, London, 1890.

14 Tasić, N., *Badanski i Vučedolski Kulturni Kompleks u Jugoslaviji*, Beograd, 1967. Jananović, B., *Starinar* XV-VI, 1964-5.

15 *Srejović, D., *ZA* VII, 1957. *Renfrew, C. *The Arts of the First Farmers*, Sheffield, 1969.

16 Korošec, J., *Glasnik Držaunog Muzeja Sarajevo*, 1945.

17 *Barfield, L. Cambridge University Library, 1968. (Ph.D. dissertation).

18 Korošec, P. *AV* 1. 1957; Battaglio, R., *BPI* (special volume on Venezia Guilia), 1958-9.

19 Bouzek, J., *Pamatky Archeologoske* LVII, 1966.

20 Garašanin, M. *Arch. Iug.* I, 1954.

21 *Gimbutas, M., *Bronze Age Cultures in Central and Eastern Europe*, The Hague, 1965. Mozsolićs, A., *BRGK* 45, 1964.

22 Korošec, P. *Arh. Porcilo* II, Ljubljana, 1963-4. Dimitrejević, S., *Sopotsko-Lengelska Kultura*, Zagreb, 1968.

23 Benac, A. *BRGK* 42, 1962. Čović, B., *BZMS* XIV, 1964.

24 Garašanin, M, *Arch Iug* 2, 1956.

25 Benac, A. and Čović, B., *Glasinac I*, Sarajevo, 1956.

26 Garašanin, D., *Starinar* IX-X, 1958-9. Tasić, N., *Starinar* XVII, 1966.

CHAPTER IV

1 *Thomas, H., Near Eastern, Mediterranean and European Chronology, *Studies in Mediterranean Archaeology* 17, 1967.

2 *Pašalić, E., *GZMS* IX, 1954.

3 For examples see Garašanin, D. *Katalog Metal Beograd* I, Beograd 1954; Benac, A., and Čović, 5., *Glasinac I*, Sarajevo 1956; Holste, F., *Hortefunde Südosteuropas*, Marburg, 1951.

4 *Piggott, S., *Ancient Europe*, Edinburgh, 1965.

5 Valmin, M., *Das Adriatische Gebiet in Vor- und-Frühbronzezeit*, Lund, 1939.

6 Condurachi, E., *Proceedings of the VII Congress of Classical Archaeology*, Paris, 1965.

7 *Sandars, N., *AJA* 67, 1963.
Foltiny, S., *MAGW* 91, 1961.

8 *Berciu, D., *Romania*, London, 1967; Popović, V. *Arch. Iug.* VI, 1967; Garašanin, M., *BRGK* 38, 1958.

9 *Childe, V., *The Danube in Prehistory*, Oxford 1929.

10 Trbuhović, V., *Problemi porekla i datovanja bronzanog doba u Srbiji*, Beograd, 1968.
*Gimbutas, M., *Bronze Age Cultures in Central and Eastern Europe*, The Hague, 1965.

11 Trbuhović, V., *Starinar* VI-VII, 1956–7.
*Sandars, N., *Prehistoric Art*, London 1968; and *Childe, V., *The Danube in Prehistory*, Oxford, 1929.

12 Truhelka, Ć., *WMBH* XII, 1904.

13 *Berciu, D., *Romania*, London, 1967.

14 Korošec, J., *GZMS*, 1946.

15 *Hammond, N., *Epirus*, Oxford, 1967.

16 *Hencken, H., *Tarquinia and Etruscan Origins*, London, 1968, with references to more detailed studies.

17 Garašanin, M., *GZMS* XIII, 1958; Benac, A. and Čović, B., *Glasinac I*, Sarajevo, 1956, Čović, B., *GZMS* XIV, 1964.

18 Truhelka, Ć., (see note 12), Marić, Z., *GZMS* XIX, 1964; Korošec, J., *GZMS* 1946; For an English summary of the original evidence see Munro, R., *Lake Dwellings of Europe*, London, 1890.

19 *Pašalić, E., *GZMS* IX, 1954.

20 *Cowen, J., *Atti VI Cong. sc. Pre- e Protohistoria Vol. II*, Florence, 1965.
Vinski, Z., and Vinski-Gasperini, K., *OA* I, 1956.

21 *Thomas, H. (note 1).
Foltiny, S., *Zur Chronologie der Bronzezeit des Karpartenbeckens*, Bonn, 1955.

22 Hoffiller, V., *Corpus Vasorum Antiquorum Yugoslavia* II, Beograd, 1934. Trbuhović, V., (note 10).

23 Holste, F., *Hortefunde Südosteuropas*, Marburg, 1951.
Vinski Z., and Vinski-Gasperini, K. *OA* I, 1956.

24 Garašanin, M and D., *La Préhistoire de la Serbie*, Beograd, 1951; *Starinar* V/VI, 1955. Garašanin, D., *Katalog Metal Beograd* I, 1954. *Invent Arch. Jug.* 2 (Y11-Y20), 1958.

25 *Heurtley, W. and Hutchinson R., *BSA* XXVII, 1926.
*Andronicos, M., *Balkan Studies* II, 1961. Garašanin, M., *Starinar* V, 1954. For a recent comment see *Hammond, N., *Epirus*, 1967.

26 Benac, A. and Čović, B., *Glasinac* I, Sarajevo, 1956; and Čović, B., *GZMS* XIV, 1964.

27 Truhelka, Ć., *WMBH* XI, 1904; Marić, Z., *GZMS* XIX, 1964; Benac, A., *GZMS* XI, 1956.

28 Buttler, W., *Prähistorische Zeitschrift*, XXIV, 1938.

29 Information from Mde. R. Dreschler-Bišić.

30 Gnirs, L. *Istria Praeromana*, Karlsbad, 1925.

31 Szombathy, J., *Mitteilungen des prähistorischen Kommission*, Wien, 11/12, 1912/13.

32 The arguments have recently been restated by *Hammond, N., *Epirus*, 1967.

33 *Hencken, K., *BASPR* 23, Cambridge U.S.A., 1968.
Sestieri, A., *BPI* 1969; Merhart, L. von, *BJ* CXLVII, 1942.

34 Foltiny, S., (Note 21).

35 *Andronicos, N., *Atti VI Cong. Sc. Pre- e Protohistoria* Florence, Vol. III. 1965. Berciu, D., *Romania*, London, 1968.

Jugoslavia

36 Gabrovec, S. *Prazgodovinske Bled,* Ljubljana, 1960.

37 Starè, F., *AV* II/I, 1950 and II/II, 1951.

38 Miroslavljević, V., *Arch. Iug.* III, 1959.

39 Richthofen, J. von, in, *Serta Hoffillieriana,* Zagreb, 1940.
Starè, F., *Invent. Arch. Iug.* I (Y1–Y10), 1957.
Hoffiller, V. (see note 22).
Bačić, B., *VAHD* LVI IX, 1954–7.

40 Marchesetti, C., *I castillierie preistorici de Trieste e Guilia,* Trieste, 1903.

41 Marović, A., *Arch. Iug.* III, 1961. Benac, A. *VAHD* 55, 1953.

42 *Alexander, J., *Antiquity* XXXVI, 1962.

43 Marić, Z., *GZMS* XIX, 1964 and XX 1965.
Čović, B., *GZMS* XIV, 1959.

CHAPTER V

1 The opening of the sea routes largely reversed the previous pattern of trade routes and cultural connections, which had all been by land.

2 *Hencken, H., Indo-European Languages and Archaeology, *American Anthropological Association* 57, 1955.
*Whatmough, J., *Pre-Italic Dialects of Italy,* Cambridge, 1953.
Gavela, B., Godošnjak III, *CBI,* 1965.
Benac, A., Simpozijum, *CBI,* 1964.
Marić, Z., *Problem sjevernog graničnog područja Ilira,* Sarajevo, 1964.

3 Garašanin, M., *ZA* X 1/2, 1960.
Merhart, L. von, *BJ* CXLVII, 1942.
Müller-Karpe, H., *Beiträge zur Chronologie der Urnenfelderzeit,* Berlin, 1959.
*Alexander, J., *Antiquity* XXXVI, 1962.

4 *Gazdapusztai, G., *Acta Archaeologica* XIX,

Buda-Pesht, 1967.

5 For examples of brooch styles: Batović, Š., *Germania* 36, 1958; *Alexander, J., *AJA* 69, 1965. Pin styles: *Jacobsthal, P., *Greek Pins,* Oxford, 1956; *Alexander, J., *PPS* XXX, 1964; Sword styles: Todorović, J., *Arch. Iug.* VI, 1965.

6 Compare the Slovene (Kromer, K., Brezje, *Arheološki Katalog Slovenska* 2, 1959) with the Croat (Urleb, M., Križna Gora, *Invent. Arch Iug.* II, (Y99–Y108) 1969) or the Bosnian (Benac, A., and Čović, B., *Glasinac II,* Sarajevo, 1957).

7 *Barfield, L., *Northern Italy,* London, 1971; Duhn, F. von, *Italienisch Gräberkunde* II, Heidelburg, 1939.

8 Marchesetti, C. *Bullettino della Soc. Adria. di Sc. Naturale,* Trieste, 1886 and 1893; Mladin, J., *Urnjetnički Spomenici prahistorijskog Nezakcija,* Pula, 1966.

9 Marchesetti, C., *I Castillieri praeistorici di Trieste e Guilia,* Trieste, 1903. Gnirs, L., *Istria Praeromana,* Karlsbad, 1925.

10 Stipčević, A., *Gli Illiri,* Milan, 1966.

11 *Beaumont, R., *Journal of Hellenic Studies* LVI, 1936.

12 Suić, M., *VAHD* 53, 1951; *Batović, Š., *Nin,* Zadar, 1968 and *Invent Arch. Iug.* (Y31–40), 1962; *Alexander, J. *Nin and the Jugoslav Iron Age,* Cambridge University Library, 1958; Vinski, Z., *Arch. Iug* 2, 1956.

13 Suić, M., Vjesnik za arheološki musej u Spitu, 1955; Batović, Š., Diadora I 1959, and *Arch. Iug* VI, 1965.

14 Novak, G., *Rad. Iug.* 322, 1961 and *Serta Hoffillieriana,* Zagreb, 1940. For a recent English summary see *Wilkes, J., *Dalmatia,* London, 1968.

15 *Alexander, J., *Antiquity* XXXVI, 1962.

16 Gabrovec, S., *Germania* 44, 1966 and *Prazgodovinski Bled,* Ljubljana, 1960.
17 *Lantier, R., in *Treasures of Carniola,* New York, 1934. Korošec, J., *Ptuj,* Ljubljana, 1951.
18 Starê, F., *Prazgodivenske Vače,* Ljubljana,. 1952 and *Ilirske najdbre ... Ljubljani,* Ljubljana, 1964. Frey, O./H., in *Symposium zu problemen der Jungeren Hallstattzeit im Mittel Europa,* Nitra, 1970.
19 *Kastelić, J., *Situla Art,* London, 1956.
20 Mirosavljević, V., *Arch. Iug.* III, 1959.
21 Dreschler-Bižić, R., *Invent Arch. Iug.* 9, 1966, and *Vjesnik Arheol. muzjea Jagrebu* 111/2, 1961; Buttler, W., *BRGK XXI* 1932.
22 *Pašalić, E., *GZMS IX,* 1954.
23 Woldrich, N. and Beck G., *WMBH V,* 1897. English account in *Munro, R., *Lake Dwellings of Europe,* London, 1890.
24 Stipčević, A., *Arte degli Illiri,* Milan, 1963. *Casson, S., *Macedonia, Illyria, Thrace,* Oxford, 1926.
25 Čović, B., *GZMS XX,* 1965; Saria, B. *Sudostforschungen* 15, 1956; Benac, A., *GZMS V,* 1952.
26 Benac, A., and Čović, B., *Glasinac II,* Sarajevo, 1957.
Pechikorn, L., *Starinar* XI, 1960.
Čović, B., Simpozijum *CBI IV,* 1964.
27 *Sandars, N., *Antiquity* XL, 1966, and *Proceedings of VII Congress Pre- and Proto-history* Vol II, Prague, 1971.
28 Truhelka, Ć., Donja Dolina der Vorges-chichtliche Pfahlbau, *WMBH IX* 1901. Marić, Z., *GZMS XIX,* 1964. Čović, B., *Invent. Arch. Iug.* 3 (Y21–30), 1961.
29 Maier, O., *Germania* XXXIV 1/2, 1956.
30 *Djuknić, M. and Janovic, B., *Illyrian Princely Necropolis at Atenica,* Cačak, 1966.
31 Gallus, S. and Horváth, J. Un Peuple cavalier présythique en Hongrie, *Disserta-tiones Pannonicae* II, Buda-Pesht, 1939.
*Gazdapusztai, G., (see note 4).
Garašanin, D., *Katalog Metal* I, Beograd, 1954.
32 Garašanin, M., *ZA* X 1/2, 1956.
33 Lahtov, V., *Problem Trebenište Kultur,* Ohrid, 1965. For the historical evidence see. *Hammond, N., *History of Greece to 322 BC,* Oxford, 1959.
34 Popović, J., *Nalaza Katalog iz Nekropole kod Trebeništa,* Beograd, 1956. Recently dis-cussed by *Hammond, N., *Epirus,* 1967. See also *Jacobsthal, P., *Greek Pins,* Oxford, 1956.
35 Petrovic, N., *Demir Kapija,* Beograd, 1961. Vučković-Todorović, J. *Starinar* IX/X, 1959.
36 *Wilkes, J., *Dalmatia,* London, 1968; Novak, G., *Serta Hoffilleriana,* Zagreb, 1940 and *Rad. Iug.* 3, 1961; Lisičar, P., *Crna Korkira,* Skopje, 1951; Abramić, M., *Egger Festschrift,* 1952.
37 Gabričević, B., *Urbs Urbanistički Biro,* Split, 1958, and *VAHD,* 1969. Suić, M., Godiš-njak III, *CBI,* 1965.
38 *Noe, S., *A Bibliography of Greek Coin Hoards,* New York, 1937. Lisičar, P. *Grčki i helenistički novci saotaka Korčule,* Zadar, 1963.
39 Sergejevski, D., Godišnjak III, *CBI,* 1965. Stipčević, A., *Arte degli Illyri,* Milan, 1963. Vasić, R., *ZA* XV, 1965.
40 *Voght, E., in *Treasures of Carniola,* New York 1934.
41 Frey, O./H., in *Dehn Festschrift.* 1969.
42 Garašanin, M., *Zbornik Matica Srpska* 18, 1957.
Gavela, B., *ŽA* I, 1951.

Jugoslavia

43 Gavela, B., *Keltski Oppidum Židovar,* Beograd, 1952. Garašanin, D., *Germania* 38, 1960. Todorović, J., Rospi Ćuprija, *Invent Arch. Iug.* 6 (Y47–56), 1963.

44 Mayer, A., in *Serta Hoffillierana,* Zagreb, 1940. Mirosaljević, V., *Arch. Iug.* III, 1959.

45 Pašaleć, E., *GZMS* IX, 1954. See also *Davies, O., *GZMS* (OS) XLIX, 1937.

46 *Lučić, J., *ZA* XVI, 1966.

47 Marić, Z., *GZMS* XVIII, 1963.

48 *Wilkes, J., *Dalmatia,* London, 1968.

Adriatica: praehistorica et antiqua (eds. Mirosavljević, D. et al), Zagreb, forthcoming.

49 Zaninović, N., and Rendic-Miočevic, D., Godiǎnijak IV, *CBI,* 1967.

50 Rendic-Miočevic, D., *OA* 4, 1959. Suić, M., Simpozijum, *CBI,* 1964.

51 *Crawford, M., *Republican Coin Hoards.*

52 Mirkovic, M. *ZA* XVIII, 1967. *Wilkes, J., (note 48) summarizes the evidence in English.

53 Garašanin, M., *Zbornik Matica Srpska* 18, 1957.

Bibliography

CLIMATE AND VEGETATION

*BUTZER, K., *Environment and Archaeology* (climate) 277 and 286, London 1965

SERCĔLJ, A., *Raz/Dis*, IX/9 (vegetation), 1966

*BEUG, H., *Review of Palaeobotany and Palynology* 2, 1967 271 (vegetation) with further references

*BONATI, E., *Nature* 209 (5027) p. 984 (vegetation)

MARKOVIĆ-MARJANOVIĆ, J., *Starinar* XI. 1960. (loes stratigraphies); *AFEQ* 1969

PALAEOLITHIC PERIOD

*VALOCH, K., *Current Anthropology* 9.5, 1968 (general background)

MILOJCIC, *Germania* 12, 1934 and 38, 1960

MAUDET, J., *Bulletin de la Societé Préhistorique Française* XLVII 431 *Germania* 36, 3/4 1958

BENAC, A., *BRGK* 1962 (Bosnia)

BASLER, D., *GZMS* XVIII 1963

BASLER, D., Brunnacker, K., and Malez, M., *GZMS* XXI-II (Bosnia) 1966-7

BRODAR, M., *Quatar* I, 1938 and 10–11, 1959 (Slovenia)

OSOLE, F., *Arheološki Pregled* 2 1960 (Slovenia)

MALEZ, M., and VUKOVIC, S., *AV* XVIII 1967 (Croatia)

MALEZ, M., *Bul Sc Yug* 5 Zagreb 1960 and 7 1962 (Dalmatia), and *Adriatica* (ed Mirosavljević, D. et al) Zagreb, forthcoming

GARAŠANIN, M., *Germania* 46.2, 1968 (rock paintings)

*DAY, M., *Guide to Fossil Man,* London 1965, with further references

ŽIVANOVIĆ, L., *Starinar* XV-VI 1964-5

MESOLITHIC PERIOD

*TRINGHAM, R., in *Studies in Ancient Europe,* ed. Coles, J. and Simpson, D., Leicester 1968, (general)

*BRUCKNER, K., *Arch. Iug.* VII, 1966 (Serbia)

*SREJOVIĆ, D., *Arch. Iug.* VII, 1966 (Lepenski Vir)

*NANDRIS, J., *Science Journal* 1968, 64 (Lepenski Vir)

RADMILLI, A., *Atti della VII Riunione Scient. nel Inst. Ital. di Prehistoria e Protohistoria* 39 1963 (Dalmatia)

ČEČUK, B., in *Adriatica : Praehistorica et Antiqua* (ed Mirosavljević, D. et al) Zagreb, forthcoming (Dalmatia)

NEOLITHIC PERIOD

General

GLIŠIĆ, J. and TRIFUNOVIĆ, L., (eds), *Les Régions Centrales des Balkans a l'Epoque neolithique,* Beograd 1968

*ERICH, R. (ed), *Chronologies in Old World Archaeology,* 1965 (for dating)

*MELLAART, J., *Antiquity* XXXIV 1960, 270–8 and Garašanin, M., *Antiquity* XXXV 1961, 276–81 (for southern connections)

BENAC, A., *BRGK* 42, 1961

Jugoslavia

Starčevo Culture

GARAŠANIN, D., *Starcevačka Kultura*, Ljubljana 1954

GALOVIĆ, R., *Die Starčevo Kultur im Jugoslavien*, Beograd 1968

BRUCKNER, D., *Neolit in Vojvodini*, Beograd-Novi Sad 1968

Vinča Culture

GARAŠANIN, M., *Hronologia Vinčanske Gruppe* Ljubljana 1951, and *Germania* 39 1961

TODOROVIĆ, J., and ČERMANOVIĆ, A., *Banjica; siedlung der Vinča gruppe*, Beograd 1961

ČOVIĆ, B., *GZMS* XV-XVI 1961

GALOVIĆ, R., *Predionica Pristina*, 1959

GARAŠANIN, M., *Arch. Iug.* III 1959, and *BRGK* 38 1958

DIMITREJEVIĆ, S., in *Simpozij Neolit i Eneolit u Slavoniji*, Vukuvar 1969

BENAC, A., *Arch. Iug.* 5 1959

Bitolj Culture

GRBIĆ, M., et al, *Neol. Tumbi Kod Bitolja* 1960

GARAŠANIN, M., *BRGK* 38 1958, and *Arch. Iug.* III 1959

Crvena Stijena Culture

BATOVIĆ, S., *Stariji Neolit u Dalmaciji*, Zadar 1966

Danilo Culture

KOROŠEC, J., *Danilo i Danilska Kultura*, Ljubljana 1964

*BRAY, W., *Antiquity*, XL 1966, 100–107

Sopot-Lengyel Culture

KOROŠEC, J., *Lengyel Kult i Bosnia, Srym e Slovenije*, Ljubljana 1957, and Drulovka, *ZFF* 111/4

DIMITREJEVIĆ, S., *Sopotsko-Lengelska Kultura*, Zagreb 1968

Butmir Culture

BENAC, A., *Neolitska naslje Nebo i problem Butmirske Kulture*, Ljubljana 1952 *BRGK* 42 1961; *GZMS* XVIII 1963 and XXI 1965

Vlasko Culture

*BARFIELD, L., *Northern Italy*, London 1971

Hvar Culture

*NOVAK, G., *Prehistoric Hvar*, Zagreb 1955

BENAC, A., and BATOVIĆ, S., in *Adriatica* (ed Mirosavlejvic et al), Zagreb forthcoming

Ljubljansko Barje Culture

*MUNRO, R., *Cave Dwellings of Europe*, London 1890

BREGANT, T., in *Porčilo o Raziskovanjci Neolita i Eneolita u Slavoniji*, Ljubljana 1964

KOROŠEC, P., *Porčila* II 1963–4

KOROŠEC, P., and J., *Najdbe s Koliščarskil naselbin pri Igu na Ljubljanskem Barju*, Ljubljana 1969

Art Forms

*SANDARS, N., *Prehistoric Art in Europe*, London 1968

SREJOVIĆ, D., *Lepenski Vir*, Belgrade 1969

BREGANT, T., *Ornamentika na Neolitski Keramiki*, Ljubljana 1968

*RENFREW, C., ed., *Arts of the First Farmers*, Sheffield 1969

EARLY METAL AGE

General

*RENFREW, C., *PPS* XXXV 1969

*THOMAS, H., *Chronologies : North-east, Mediterranean, European* 1, Lund 1967 108

*GIMBUTAS, M., *Bronze Age Cultures in Central and Eastern Europe*, Hague 1965

PASSEK, T., in *Europe à la fin de l'age de la pierre* (eds Soudsky, B. and Plesova, E.) Prague 1961

TRBUHOVIĆ, L., *Problem Porekla i Datovanja Bronzanog Dobe u Srbiji*, Beograd 1968
Simpoziji: neolit eneolit u Slavoniji, (Dimitrejević, S. ed.) Vukuvar 1969
Porčilo o Raziskovanjci Neolita in Eneolita v Sloveniji, Ljubljana 1964

POPOVIĆ, V., *Arch. Iug.* VI 1965

GARAŠANIN, M., *BRGK* 1958 (Serbia and Macedonia)

Baden-Pecel, Kostolac, Lasinja Cultures

SREJOVIĆ, D., *Arch. Iug.* IV 1963

DIMITREJEVIĆ, S., *Arh Rad* 2 1962 (Baden)

TASIĆ, N., *Arch. Iug.* VII 1966 (Kostolac) and *Badenski i Vucedolski Kulturni Kompleks u Jugoslaviji*, Beograd 1967

JANOVIĆ, B., *Starinar* XV-VI 1964–5

BENAC, A., *BRGK* 42 1962

Slavonian-Vučedol Culture

SCHMIDT, R., *Die Burg Vučedol*, Zagreb 1945

TASIĆ, N., (op cit)

Bubanj-Hum Culture

GARAŠANIN, M., *Germania* 35 1957, *Arch. Iug.* I 1954, and *PZ* 35 1958

Sopot-Lengyel Culture

DIMITREJEVIĆ, S., *Sopotsko-Lengelska Kultura* Zagreb 1968

Early Tumulus Cultures

GARAŠANIN, M. and D., *GZMS* XIII. 1958 and *Arch. Iug.* 2 1956 (W. Serbia)

BENAC, A., and ČOVIĆ, B., *Glasinac I,* Sarajevo 1956

Slatina-Paračin Culture

GARAŠANIN, D., *Starinar* X-XI 1958–9

Adriatic Coasts

*NOVAK, G., *Prehistoric Hvar,* Zagreb

BATTAGLIA, R., *BPI*, special volume on *Venezia Giulia* 1958–9

*BARFIELD, L., *Northern Italy*, London 1971 (for Brijuni-Skočjan group)

KOROŠEC, P., *AV* VI 1957

LATER BRONZE AGE
General

*THOMAS, H., *Studies in Mediterranean Archaeology* 17 Lund 1967

*GIMBUTAS, M., *Bronze Age Cultures in Central and Eastern Europe,* Hague 1965 (with earlier references) 345f

FOLTINY, S., *Zur Chronologie der Bronzezeit des Karpartenbeckens*, Bonn 1955

*COWAN, J., *Atti VI Congresso pre e protoistoria*, Florence 1966

*SANDARS, N., *AJA LXVII* 1963, 117–53

West Serbian and Bosnian Tumulus Cultures

GARAŠANIN, M. and D., *GZMS* XIII 1958

BENAC, A., and ČOVIĆ, B., *Glasinac I and II,* Sarajevo 1956 and 1957, (modified by Čović, B., *GZMS* XVIII 1963)

MARIC, Z., *GZMS* XIV-V 1961 (Donja Dolina) with earlier references, also

TRUHELKA, C., Pfahlbau bei Donja Dolina, *WMBH* IX Vienna 1904

Urnfield Cultures

DIMITREJEVIĆ, S., *Proceedings XI Congress Science and History*, Stockholm 1960

*CHILDE, V., *The Danube in Prehistory*, Oxford 1929, 284 ff.

GARAŠANIN, M., *Starinar* V-VI 1954

Jugoslavia

*HENCKEN, H., Tarquinia, Villanovans and Etruscans, *BASPR* 23 1968

Croatia

HOFFILLER, V., *Corpus Vasorum Antiquarum* II, Zagreb 1934

VINSKI, Z., and VINSKI-GASPARINI, K., *Opuscula Arheologica* I 1956

Slovenia

STARÈ, F., *AV* II/I 1950, II/II 1951 and *Inventaria Arch. Iug.* 1 1957

GABROVEC, S., *Germania* 44 1966, *Prazgodovinske Bled,* Ljubljana 1960

Dalmatia and Istria

BAČIĆ, B., *VAHD*, LVI-IX 1957

MARIĆ, Z., *GZMS* XIX 1964; XX 1965

MAROVIĆ, M., *Arch. Iug.* IV 1961

Serbia

GARAŠANIN, D., *Katalog Metal Beograd I*, Beograd 1954

Art Styles

TRBUHOVIĆ, V., *Starinar* VI-VII 1956-7

BOSKOVIC, D., *Arch. Iug.* 3 1959 (Dupljaja chariot)

*SĂNDARS, N., *Prehistoric Art*, London 1968

ZAGORKA, L., *Starinar* XIX 1968

IRON AGE

General

*SANDARS, N., *Antiquity,* XXXVIII, 1964, 258–61 and *Actes du VII Congrès Int. des Sciences Préhistoriques et Protohistoriques* Prague 1971

*ALEXANDER, J., *Antiquity* XXXVI 1962, 123–30

*GAZDAPUSZTAI, G., *Acta Archaeologica* XIX Buda-Pesht 1967

BENAC, A. (ed.), Kulture Ilira Simpozium, *CBI* 4 Sarajevo

STIPČEVIĆ, A., *Gli Illyri*, Milan 1966

*CASSON, S., *Macedonia, Illyria, Thrace,* Oxford 1926 (summary of earlier finds)

Slovenia

GABROVIC, S., *Germania* 44 1966 and *Prazgodovinske Bled,* Ljubljana 1960

STARÈ, F., *Prazgodovinske Vače, Ljubljana* 1952 and *Actes VII Congrès,* Prague 1971
Treasures of Carniola, New York 1934 (for older evidence)

MÜLLER-KARPE, H., *Beiträge zur Chronologie der Urnenfelderzeit,* Berlin 1959

Bosnia-Hercegovina

BENAC, A., and ČOVIĆ, B., *Glasinac II*, Sarajevo 1957 (with older references)

ČOVIĆ, B., *GZMS* 20 1965 and *Inventaria Arch. Iug.* 3 1961

PASALIC, E., *GZMS* IX 1964

*CASSON, S. (op cit)

Dalmatia

*WILKES, J., *Dalmatia*, London 1968 (with older references)

BAČIĆ, B., in Mirosavljević, V. et al (eds) *Adriatica : Praehistorica et Antiqua*, Zagreb forthcoming

BATOVIĆ, Š., *Germania* 36 1958, and *NIN*, Zadar 1968

LISICAR, D., *Crna Korkira,* Skoplje 1951

MLADIN, J., *Urnjetnicki Spomenici pra. Nezakcija*, Pula 1966

Croatia

MIROSAVLJEVIĆ, V., *Arch. Iug.* III 1959

DRESCHLER-BIŽIĆ, R., *Inventaria Arch. Iug.* 9 1966

Serbia

TODOROVIĆ, J., Rospi Cuprija, *Inventaria Arch. Iug.* 6 1963

GARAŠANIN, M., *Germania* 38 1960, and *ZM* 18 1957

GAVELA, B., *Keltski Oppidum Židovar,* Beograd 1952

*DJUKNIC, M., and NOVANOVIĆ, R., *Illyrian Princely Necropolis at Atenica,* Čicak 1966

GARAŠANIN, M., *ZA,* X 1–2 1956 *II,* Beograd 1954 and 1958

Macedonia

GARAŠANIN, M., *ZX* 1–2 1956

LATOV, V., *Problem Trebenište Kultur,* Ohrid 1965

POPOVIĆ, J., *Nalaza Katalog iz Nekropole kod Trebenište,* Beograd 1956

PETROVIĆ, N., *Demir Kapja,* Beograd 1961

Art Styles

STIPČEVIĆ, A., *Arte degli Illyri,* Milan 1963

SERGEJEVSKI, D., in *CBI* III Sarajevo 1965

*KASTELIĆ J., *Situla Art,* London 1965

GENERAL BOOKS IN SERBO CROAT

GARAŠANIN, M., and KOVAČEVIĆ, J., *Arheološki Nalazi u Jugoslaviji,* Beograd 1962

GAVELA, B., *Praistoriska Arheologija,* Beograd 1969

SOURCES OF THE PLATES

Grateful acknowledgement is made to the following persons and institutions who have provided illustrations and permission to publish them:

Ashmolean Museum, Oxford 46; Birmingham City Museum 9; A. Belić 47, 50; British Museum 52–5; R. Dreschler-Bižić and the Archaeological Museum, Zagreb 34, 35, 36. O.-H. Frey 49; D. Garašanin and the National Museum, Zagreb 18, 28; P. Hameljak 48; A. Kastelić and the Archaeological Museum, Ljubljana 44, 45; J. Powell and N. Sandars, 10–13, 24, 27, 29, 40, 51 (National Museum, Beograd); 15, 42, 47 (Archaeological Museum Sarajevo); 16, 17, 21, 22, 25, 26, 37, 41 (Archaeological Museum, Zagreb); Osijek Museum 30; J. Scott and the Priština Museum 14, 32; D. Srejović 5–8; V. Starè and the Archaeological Museum, Ljubljana 1, 2, 19, 20, 38; J. Weiner and M. Day 3, 4.

Acknowledgments

It is a pleasure to record my gratitude for the help, spread over many years, which has made this book possible. My debt to Professor and Mde. Korošec is acknowledged in the dedication, but I am also under great obligation to Professor and Mde. Starè of Ljubljana University and Museum, Drs M. and D. Garašanin of the Jugoslav Academy of Arts and Sciences and Beograd Museum, and Professor M. Suić, Dr Z. Vinski and Mde R. Dreschler-Bižić of Zagreb University and Museum.

For reading and commenting on parts of the text I am grateful to Drs L. Barfield and R. Tringham; Messrs J. Brownfield, A. Harding, A. Sharratt and P. Woudhuysen, Mrs V. Morton, D. Radulović-Jenkins; Miss P. Harris and Miss N. Sandars.

The maps and drawings were executed by Mr David Eccles and Miss G. D. Jones respectively and the index by Miss Betty Powell. Thanks and acknowledgements of the photographs are given separately but I would like to thank Miss N. Sandars in particular for her help with them.

A special word of appreciation is also due to Mrs J. Hartley and Mr P. Clayton of Thames and Hudson for their patience and aid during publication.

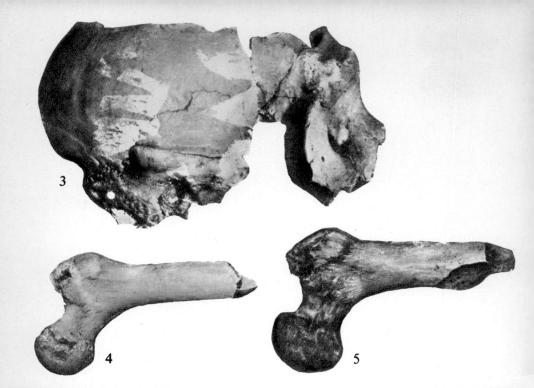

8

9

10

11

12

13

15

14

16

17

18

19

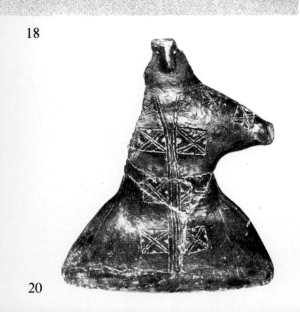

20

21

22

23

24

25

26

27

28

29

30

31

32

33

34

35

36

37

38

39

40

41

42

43

44

45, 46   47

48

49

50

51

52

53

54

55

Notes on the Plates

1 Betulov Spodmol (Slovenia). Cave in lime-stone *Karst* country. The 14 m. of stratified remains contained evidences of human occupation from Middle Palaeolithic to Medieval times.

2 Potočka Zijalka (Slovenia). A cave, similar to that shown in Plate 1, during excavation, showing here the Late Pleistocene (Würm) deposits which contained a succession of Upper Palaeolithic industries.

3, 4 Krapina (Croatia). Skull and thighbone fragments from the rock-shelter where at least 13 men, women and children were found in levels belonging to the end of the last Interglacial. They have been described as 'generalised Neanderthalers' but are very little different from modern man.

5 Lepenski Vir (Serbia). Globular pot of Starčevo culture type, characteristic of the earliest farming settlements in Serbia.

6 One of the fifty-four sculptured boulders found in the hunter-fisher levels of the settlement of Lepenski Vir and dating from the fifth millennium BC.

7 Lepenski Vir: general view from the site showing its situation on a small terrace within the Danubian Gates.

8 A grave showing one of the rare and distinctive burials at Lepenski Vir

9 Vinča (Serbia). A view of the excavation of the 9 m. accumulation of settlement debris beside the Danube. It shows the rolling, loess-covered countryside much liked by early farmers.

10 Bust of a clay figure from Vinča, in Srejović's 'Free Realistic' style; note the hat. Vinča-Tordos Culture.

11 Butmir (Bosnia). Head of a clay figure from the neolithic settlement. The modelling and hair style are very different from the Vinča figures.

12 Vinča (Serbia). Vase in human shape with arms perforated for suspension, Renfrew's 'Priština' style. Note the conventionalized face and the body decoration. Vinča-Pločnik Culture.

13 Jar and lid from Vinča in another Vinča-Pločnik style. The incised linear and in-filled stab ornament has parallels in the neolithic of Central Europe and the 'owl' lid in the south.

14 Priština (Serbia). Beautifully modelled clay head in the full Priština style. The treatment of the eyes, eyebrows and nose is particularly distinctive. Vinča-Pločnik Culture.

15 Butmir (Bosnia) Bowl of the Butmir Culture. The carefully grooved ornament, often encrusted in red or white, shows contact

between Bosnia and the Adriatic coasts in neolithic times.

16 Left, Sarvaš (Croatia). Cups of Baden Culture origin. Note the high necks and strap handles. Right, Vučedol (Croatia). Vase in the shape of a boot. Slavonian-Vučedol Culture. See costume reconstruction in fig. 30.

17 Rumal (Serbia). Cup of the Baden Culture, perhaps from a leather prototype. Late third —early second millennium BC.

18 Srpski Krstur (Serbia). Vase with impressed cord ornament showing northern connections. Late third—early second millennium BC.

19 Ig (Slovenia). Clay figurine of the Ljubljansko Barje Culture. Note the incised and encrusted ornament which probably indicates clothing.

20 Vase (in the shape of a pair of trousers?) from the same culture as the figurine in Plate 19. The ornament shows connection with the Slavonian-Vučedol Culture of Croatia.

21, 22 Sarvaš (Croatia). Pottery of the Slavonian-Vučedol Culture. The excised patterns suggest those of woodcarving. Similar patterns are still in use in the country today.

23 Vučedol (Croatia). Vase in the form of a stylised bird, perhaps from a leather model. Note the stitch ornament on the neck. Slavonian-Vučedol Culture.

24 Mokrin (Serbia). Vase of the Periam Culture.

25 Surčin (Serbia). Vase of Middle Danubian Urnfield type usually found in cremation cemeteries. Note the impressed and incised ornament.

26 Vase from Surčin with excised ornament sometimes described as an amphora; Vattina Culture. Note the concentration of ornament on the neck. Late second millennium BC.

27 Omoljica (Serbia). Cup with an ornamented stud on the handle.

28 Dupljaja (Serbia). Clay chariot drawn by waterbirds, in the 'Kličevac' art style (for reconstruction see Fig. 42). Dubovac-Žuto brdo Culture. Mid second millennium.

29 Omoljica (Serbia). 'Amphora' with peaked rim and handles of Vattina style, notable for the fluting on the body and the fine burnishing. Mid second millennium BC.

30 Bijelo Brdo (Croatia). Two-storeyed vase, with white encrusted ornament, of a type found in urnfield cemeteries of the Osjek region. Late second millennium BC.

31 Vukovar (Croatia). Late Bronze Age vase showing raised burnished ornament which probably copies a metal prototype.

32 Croatia. 'Posamentarie' fibula of Middle Danube type, common in Hungary but derived from further north. Early first millennium BC.

33 Prozor (Croatia). View of the important and well-defended Iron Age settlement and its cemeteries; the rampart is visible on the nearest hill, the cemeteries are below it. Note the countryside typical of the valleys behind the coastal mountains.

34 Makujak (Croatia). View of the tumbled stone wall of a hill-fort in *karst* country.

35 Urebac (Croatia). Large 'contour' hill-fort (oppidum) of the Early Iron Age in the Lika Valley.

36 Strpči (Slovenia). View during the excavation of a very large Iron Age burial mound showing the stone retaining wall. Eighth/seventh century BC.

37 Dalj (Croatia). An 'animal rhyton' (cup for pouring libations) and 'dipper', the latter probably copying a metal form. Eighth/seventh century BC.

38 Podzemelj (Slovenia). Vase from a Slovene urnfield of the the earliest Iron Age. Notice the similarities with the Croatian urns.

39 Ljubljana (Slovenia). A 'bird rhyton' from the S.A.Z.U. (Early Iron Age) cemetery.

40 Curug (Serbia). Fibula in the form of a snake and related to the Strbči type. Widespread in southern Jugoslavia and beyond. Found in this hoard with La Tène fibulae of the fourth/third century BC.

41 Prozor (Croatia). Bronze pendant in the form of an animal (?dog). Models of this kind become commoner after the seventh century BC.

42 Donja Dolina (Bosnia). Horse-bit with cheek-pieces in the form of horses' or cows' heads from the riverside settlement. Probably related to Central Italian types of the late eighth/seventh centuries.

43 Jeserine (Bosnia). Part of a bronze and amber brooch found in a grave with La Tène fibulae of the third/second centuries.

44 Vače (Slovenia). Part of a bronze beltplate in repoussée ornament showing cavalry fighting. Note the type of battle axe and helmet in use. Seventh century BC.

45 A similar fragment, showing a well-armed foot soldier of the period.

46 Situla or bucket of bronze from grave 3, Barrow I at Vače. The repoussée ornament is Italian style of the seventh/sixth century BC.

47 Trebenište (Macedonia). Bronze helmet of Greek style with applied gold disc, and stud and grooves for a crest. From the royal cemetery of the late sixth century.

48 Sheet gold death mask from another grave in the cemetery at Trebenište.

49 Vače (Slovenia). Bronze situla from Barrow I with repoussée ornament in the Italian 'Bologna' style of the late sixth century.

50 Grajasnica (Macedonia). Terracotta figure of 'Tanagra' type, probably an import from northern Greece.

Jugoslavia

51 Mramorac (Serbia). Silver belt with fine geometric ornament on the wider terminal. Found together with a gold bracelet possibly in a grave of the sixth/fifth century BC.

52 Bronze coin of the mainland Greek city of Herakleia, of the fourth century BC. *Obverse*, the head of Herakles wearing the lion's skin and, *reverse*, his bow and club.
Weight 16.71 grams.

53 Bronze coin of the Greek colony on Issa (Viš), of the third century BC. *Obverse*, the helmeted head of Athena and, *reverse*, a goat.
Weight 7.56 grams.

54 Bronze coin of the Greek colony on Pharos; fourth century BC. *Obverse*, the head of Sens; *reverse*, a goat.
Weight 18.70 grams.

Index

Page numbers in *italic* refer to illustrations in text.